An Associate's First Year

An Associate's First Year

A Guide to Thriving at a Law Firm

Edited by

Jennifer L. Bluestein

Global Director of Professional
Development & Training,
Greenberg Traurig LLP

Practising Law Institute • New York City • #256411

This work is designed to provide practical and useful information on the subject matter covered. However, it is sold with the understanding that neither the publisher nor the author is engaged in rendering legal, accounting, or other professional services. If legal advice or other expert assistance is required, the services of a competent professional should be sought.

QUESTIONS ABOUT THIS BOOK?

If you have questions about billing or shipments, or would like information on our other products, please contact our **customer service department** at info@pli.edu or at (800) 260-4PLI.

For any other questions or suggestions about this book, contact PLI's **editorial department** at plipress@pli.edu.

For general information about Practising Law Institute, please visit **www.pli.edu**.

Legal Editor: Lori Wood

LCCN: 2018961288

ISBN: 978-1-4024-3271-2

About the Editor

Jennifer L. Bluestein (Chapter 2) is a strategic talent development leader. She is a thinker, an executor, and a leader when it comes to recruiting, retaining, compensating, and elevating talent at all levels, particularly at law firms. Jennifer has been the Director of Global Professional Development & Training at Greenberg Traurig LLP since 2008. She worked in human resources both before law school and after practicing labor and employment law at two large law firms in Chicago. After working as a human resources consultant for RSM McGladrey, Jennifer joined a global law firm as its first Director of Professional Development. She was Chair of the Professional Development Consortium (PDC) from 2011–2013 and Co-Chair of the Alliance for Women of the Chicago Bar Association from 2009–2010, where she also served as a liaison to the ABA Commission on Women. Jennifer received her J.D. from Northwestern University School of Law in 1996 and her B.A. from Tufts University.

About the Contributors

Dr. Sharon Meit Abrahams (Chapter 17) is a legal talent development expert helping lawyers improve their productivity and profitability. She currently serves as Director, Professional Development/Diversity & Inclusion for the international law firm, Foley & Lardner LLP. She has conducted over 170 seminars on a wide variety of topics. Her audience has been the American Bar Association (ABA), local bar associations, the Association of Legal Administrators (regional and national), and Harvard, Yale, Cornell, Northwestern, University of Virginia, University of Chicago, and Duke Law Schools. Dr. Abrahams is a prolific writer, publishing over sixty articles and three books related to professional development in the legal profession. She was on the faculty for the Center for Management Development at Florida International University and an adjunct professor in the doctoral program "Organizational Leadership" at Nova Southeastern University. Dr. Abrahams has a Bachelor's of Business Administration and a Master's of Science in Instructional Technology/Organizational Training from the University of Miami and a doctorate in Adult Education from Nova Southeastern University. She gives back to the local and legal community by offering programming on a cost-free basis to nonprofit organizations.

Chintan Amin (Chapter 9) is an in-house attorney for Bayer, one of the largest life sciences companies in the world. At Bayer, he is responsible for environmental, health and safety issues, real estate, and political activity law. He is also a past Executive Committee member of the South Asian Bar Association of North America. Prior to joining Bayer, Chintan practiced environmental law for over eleven years as an associate and partner with the Atlanta office of Kilpatrick Stockton LLP (now Kilpatrick Townsend & Stockton LLP). Chintan graduated with High Honors from the University of Florida, Levin College of Law, where he served on the editorial board of the *Florida Journal of International Law*. He also holds a B.S. in Materials Science and Engineering from the University of Illinois Urbana-Champaign.

Josephine Bae (Chapter 5) is an associate in Baker McKenzie's Chicago office. She advises clients on a range of global and domestic mergers and acquisitions, corporate reorganizations and other strategic transactions. Josephine received her J.D. from Columbia Law School and B.S. from the School of Foreign Service at Georgetown University

Sandra Bang (Chapter 4) is the Chief Diversity and Talent Strategy Officer at the international law firm, Shearman & Sterling LLP, and leads the diversity and inclusion, professional development, legal recruitment, and partner and counsel services teams and initiatives. Originally from Canada, Sandra began her legal career as a litigation lawyer. She has been passionate about talent management and career coaching for over seventeen years and has worked at several different law firms in Canada and the United States.

Chris Boyd (Chapter 8) is the Chief Knowledge and Talent Officer for Wilson Sonsini Goodrich & Rosati in Palo Alto, California. Chris leads the firm's attorney recruiting, diversity, knowledge management, professional development, research and information services, and work allocation professionals. They work with firm and practice group leaders to develop, deploy, and continuously improve recruiting and integration processes, talent management programs, and practice support tools that support the firm's business goals and help the firm deliver more value to clients. Chris has an undergraduate degree from Princeton University and a law degree from Stanford Law School. Before his current role, he worked as a management consultant, corporate and securities attorney, and technology company knowledge management leader. He is a member of the Board of Directors of the International Legal Technology Association and is a Fellow of the College of Law Practice Management.

Esther Chang (Chapters 11 and 12) is a Corporate & Securities associate in Mayer Brown's Chicago office. Esther focuses her practice on mergers and acquisitions, advising both public and private companies on cross-border and domestic mergers, acquisitions and divestitures, corporate governance, general corporate and business law. Esther was named a Rising Star by *Illinois Super Lawyers* between 2014 and 2017 for mergers and acquisitions. Esther speaks Mandarin and is proficient in French.

Grover E. Cleveland (Chapter 3) is a sought-after speaker on law career success and the author of *Swimming Lessons for Baby Sharks: The Essential Guide to Thriving as a New Lawyer.* Published by West Academic, the book is in its Second Edition and includes a Foreword by Mark Weber, Assistant Dean for Career Services, Harvard Law School. Grover provides interactive practical skills workshops for AmLaw200 firms and select coaching engagements for high-performing lawyers. Grover's workshops focus on actionable skills to help lawyers build trust, become fully engaged in practice, and provide more value sooner. Coaching engagements help established lawyers take their practices to the next level. Grover is a former partner at Foster Pepper PLLC, one of the larger law firms in the Northwest. His clients included the Seattle Seahawks professional football team as well as other companies owned by Microsoft co-founder, Paul Allen. Grover is also a regular speaker at national career conferences, and he writes a widely read career advice column for lawyers. His columns appear in numerous blogs and publications, including Above the Law, Ms. JD, and American Bar Association sites. He was named after his grandfather, who was named after the 22nd and 24th President of the United States. There is no blood relationship.

Anne Collier (Chapter 15) is the chief operating officer of Arudia, a firm dedicated to improving culture, collaboration, and communication. She practiced law for over a decade, starting her career as a tax lawyer at the Internal Revenue Service, Office of Chief Counsel and at Legislative Affairs, and then moving to private practice. In 2002, she ceased practicing law and began supporting clients in developing more fulfilling personal lives and careers via career and executive coaching as well as working with teams and enterprise-wide. She also supports individuals and groups in improving resilience and reducing reactivity through greater self-awareness, communication tools, and tailored strategies, and develops others' leadership, management, and collaboration skills. She is a sought-after speaker. Anne has her J.D. from the University of Michigan, *cum laude*, her Master of Public Policy from the Institute of Public Policy Studies (now the Gerald R. Ford School of Public Policy) at the University of Michigan, and is an ICF Professional Certified Coach.

Catharine Du Bois (Chapters 10 and 13) is a legal writing consultant offering seminars and individual coaching. She recently joined the Legal Practice faculty at New York Law School as a visiting professor. Her expertise is in legal skills, specifically advocacy and persuasive writing. Catharine began teaching legal writing in 2008 when she left practice to join the faculty at the University of Colorado Law School. She has been teaching both students and lawyers ever since. Before moving to New York, at Indiana University Bloomington she taught Legal Writing and Research at the Maurer School of Law and taught Law and Public Policy at the School of Public and Environmental Affairs. Catharine is also a Program Director at the National Institute for Trial Advocacy (NITA) where she teaches seminars in Persuasive Writing. Catharine is a graduate of Georgetown Law School. She practiced in the litigation departments of Jenner & Block LLP, Chicago, and Jones Day, New York, and clerked for the Honorable Steven D. Merryday of the U.S. District Court for the Middle District of Florida.

Aria Eckersley (Chapter 5) is an associate in Baker McKenzie's Corporate & Securities Practice Group in Chicago. Aria advises multinational companies on global and domestic transactional matters, including mergers and acquisitions, corporate reorganizations and other strategic transactions. Prior to joining Baker McKenzie, Aria was a student clinician at the University of Chicago Kirkland & Ellis Corporate Lab as well as the Institute for Justice Clinic on Entrepreneurship. Aria received her Bachelor's degree in English and Political Science from the University of Illinois at Chicago and her Juris Doctor degree from the University of Chicago Law School.

Amy Halverson (Chapter 8) is Director of Knowledge Management, Research & Information Services at Wilson Sonsini Goodrich & Rosati. An attorney and former litigator, she focuses on the creation of firm-wide knowledge-sharing and collaboration systems that increase the value provided by firms to clients and advance the business and practice of law. Amy initially left private practice to direct the online editorial operations of a national legal news and information website. She then returned to the law firm environment, where she calls upon her legal and technical experience to facilitate the development of tools that capitalize on existing law firm information flows and business processes. An active member of the

California State Bar, she is a graduate of UC Hastings College of the Law and of UCLA.

Brad D. Kaufman (Chapter 1) is a Senior Vice President and Treasurer of Greenberg Traurig. He is also Co-Chair of the Securities Litigation Group and Global Chairman of the firm's Professional Development and Integration. He focuses his practice on securities litigation and regulatory actions. He has represented major broker/dealers, investment banks, and investment advisors in all aspects of their business, including traditional litigation in state and federal court as well as arbitrations. Brad has defended both securities class actions and shareholder derivative claims. He has appeared as counsel in securities cases in most of the Federal Circuit courts in the United States as well as before the U.S. Supreme Court. Brad has been listed as a "Top Lawyer" by the *South Florida Legal Guide* from 2009–2013 and has been selected by *Super Lawyers* magazine since 2006. He is rated AV® Preeminent™ 5.0 out of 5* and has been listed in *Best Lawyers in America* from 2008–2014. Brad was also listed in *Chambers & Partners USA Guide*, an annual listing of the leading business lawyers and law firms in the world, from 2007–2008. He frequently speaks at Securities Litigation and Arbitration Conferences, including the Practising Law Institute, the American Conference Institute, and many others. Brad received his J.D. from Stetson University College of Law and his B.S. from Florida State University.

Julie E. LaEace (Chapter 7) is Pro Bono Counsel and Director of Pro Bono at Kirkland & Ellis. She joined the firm in 2007. Prior to joining Kirkland, Julie practiced employment law and employee benefits at two Chicago firms before transitioning to law firm management. In her pro bono role, Julie is responsible for leading and overseeing the firm's global pro bono practice, including project development, recognition programming, marketing, risk management, and other administration.

Since she became the first pro bono professional at the firm, attorney participation in pro bono has grown by 133% and the firm's pro bono hours have increased by more than 60%. Julie is a 1998 *magna cum laude* graduate of Notre Dame Law School and received a B.S. degree in Business Economics from Indiana University in 1995. She has served in volunteer advisory and leadership roles for various nonprofit organizations.

Julie Lehrman (Chapter 18) is a longtime Legal Recruiter and is a Founding Member of North Star Attorney Search, LLC. She regularly places attorneys nationally with law firms and in-house legal departments of all sizes, and has also facilitated mergers. In addition to having over ten years' legal recruiting experience, Julie also practiced law at two AmLaw100 firms and was Assistant Counsel at a major national labor organization. She earned her J.D. from Georgetown University Law Center, where she was a Senior Editor on the school's law review, the *Georgetown Law Journal*. After law school, she served as a Judicial Law Clerk for the Honorable John M. Steadman of the District of Columbia Court of Appeals, and then for the Honorable Hilda G. Tagle on the United States District Court for the Southern District of Texas. Her B.A., in French and Comparative Literature, is from Washington University.

Serena Miller (Chapter 8) is the Director of Professional Development at Wilson Sonsini Goodrich & Rosati. Prior to joining WSGR in 2016, Serena worked as a talent management expert and professional skills coach and has over twenty years of practical knowledge in the design, implementation, and administration of attorney development programs. She has created, implemented, torn apart, and rebuilt programs for onboarding/orientation, interpersonal skills, management skills, leadership skills, mentoring, succession planning, diversity and inclusion programming, competencies, and evaluations with both in-house and consulting perspectives. Serena is also a certified administrator of both the DiSC and Myers-Briggs inventories. Serena began her career as an assistant district attorney in Brooklyn, New York and is a graduate of the University of Texas and the City University of New York School of Law.

Laura S. Norman (Chapter 16) is an attorney with over thirty-five years of experience. Early in her career she was a lecturer in law at Columbia University School of Law and until recently was a shareholder at the international law firm, Greenberg Traurig. She is currently a professional development consultant and President of LSN Consulting Ltd. and manages professional development for the New York, New Jersey, and White Plains offices of Greenberg Traurig.

Jane DiRenzo Pigott (Chapter 6) is Managing Director of R3 Group LLC and specializes in providing leadership, change, and talent consulting to organizations through a focus on the retention, development, and promotion of talent. Before starting R3 Group, Jane practiced law for over twenty years, most recently at Winston & Strawn where she served as the Chair of the global Environmental Law practice. At Winston, she served on the firm's Executive Management Committee, the first woman to do so, and on its Compensation Committee. Jane also serves on a number of business and civic boards.

Elizabeth Roque (Chapter 5) is an associate in the Corporate & Securities Practice Group in Baker McKenzie's Chicago office. Elizabeth advises multinational companies on transactional matters, including domestic and cross-border mergers and acquisitions and corporate reorganizations. Elizabeth received her Bachelor's degree from Drake University and her Juris Doctor degree from the University of Chicago Law School.

Annapoorni (Anna) Sankaran (Chapter 14) is a partner in the litigation practice at Holland & Knight in Houston. She focuses her practice on a variety of commercial litigation matters, with an emphasis on bankruptcy and bankruptcy litigation. Anna represents institutional and individual clients in all stages of business disputes. She has trial and appellate experience before federal and state courts, and represents clients in mediation and arbitration. Anna has won appeals in the First, Third, Fourth, Fifth, and Ninth Circuit Courts of Appeal of the United States, as well as in Massachusetts and Texas appeals courts. She was awarded the Silver Shingle Award for Service to the Profession by Boston University School of Law in 2017 and has been on the "40 Under 40" lists for the *Business Journals* of two different cities, Boston and Houston. In her free time, Anna does stand-up comedy and can be found at various comedy clubs when she isn't on trial.

Olivia Tyrrell (Chapter 5) is a Corporate/M&A partner in Baker McKenzie's Chicago office. Olivia has also practiced in the firm's Sydney and Barcelona offices. She is a member of Baker McKenzie's Global Transactional Healthcare group. Olivia received the "Chicago 40 Under 40" award from the *National Law Journal* and was named among the "most influential women lawyers in Chicago in 2017" by *Crain's Chicago Business*.

Table of Chapters

Table of Contents

Table of Contents

Preface

I still remember the first time I really gained a sense of how challenging the first year of practicing law can be for new attorneys. I had just begun my second year of practice, and I went out to dinner with an associate who was one year ahead of me. She listened as I told her about how I was looking back at all the things I did not know coming out of law school. "I can't believe how much I didn't learn in law school," I told her. And my friend replied, "Welcome to your first year of law practice. You survived!"

It was a difficult year because I didn't even know what I didn't know until faced with an assignment that made me feel like I had just wasted three years and many thousands of dollars on law school. I constantly felt lost and over-worked. I couldn't even read fiction because I was so tired at the end of every day. And yet, after one year or so, things just started to click. I realized that little by little, I knew what the partner or senior associate wanted when she or he assigned me something. I could anticipate the next step in a matter before being asked. I was able to come up with novel approaches to cases that seemed to have no winning argument. That was when I knew I was a lawyer. It wasn't when I graduated; it wasn't when I was sworn in. It was when I knew what to do next without being instructed. That was a beautiful realization. I had gone from deciphering the Rule Against Perpetuities and The Mailbox Rule to drafting a Summary Judgment Motion that could be filed without having ten rounds of red-inked revisions.

As a result, my confidence grew immensely. As I see the new attorneys around me, what separates the aspiring associates from the star associates is their confidence. They know they can do it, and so they do. I hope this book will help you, our readers, acquire this confidence quickly. Your level of confidence will make your career a successful one, and it will help bring satisfaction with your chosen position. But if it doesn't, this book is also designed to help you understand what to do next. Get to know yourself and play to your strengths, and if you find that the daily practice of law isn't what drives you, find the confidence to explore something else. And have fun whatever you do!

JENNIFER L. BLUESTEIN
October 2018
Chicago, Illinois

Acknowledgments

Many people spent a lot of time to make this book become a reality. I would like to thank Lori Wood at PLI for spending the time to consider every word and nuance in every chapter. She has been a wonderful editor and a real value-add in the best way. And of course, PLI's support and risk-taking to enter into the new associates space shows a true dedication to the profession and new attorneys everywhere.

Thanks also goes out to each and every author in this book, because the time they each took to translate their knowledge into readable form was significant. Greenberg Traurig and Brad Kaufman were both completely supportive of this project, which I truly appreciate. And finally, I want to thank my family for their constant support, from my husband, Mike Fink, bringing me coffee in bed, to my daughter, Jaxanna, helping me decide where I needed an extra comma, and my son, Bennett, cracking a joke to end my cranky mood. My parents, Maris and Maurice Bluestein, each set an example by publishing their own books, and my sister, Karen Bluestein, edited many books over the course of her career. Now the pressure moves on to my brother, Richard!

Finally, to the readers of this book, thanks to each of you for attending law school and continuing to believe in the legal justice system despite some tumultuous times. Always remember that you are an officer of the court, and it is a privilege to understand the law and have access to it. It is our role to share that access with others.

Chapter 1

Expectations of a First Year

Brad D. Kaufman[*]

You've done it—you've made it through law school; you've taken the bar exam, and you even got a little time off before starting your full-time job as an associate. Congratulations! You've made it through the hardest part.

About 55 million students attend public or private elementary schools through grade 12 during any given year. In 2011, 83% of high school students graduated in the United States, or 3.1 million. This number was 3.6 million for 2018.[1]

Of those 3.1 million in 2011, 2.1 million enrolled in college, roughly 70%. Of those 2.1 million, about 59% graduated from college, approximately 1.25 million. Of those, about 37,000 matriculated to an ABA-accredited U.S. law school. And of the class of 2017, 23,000 graduated with full-time long-term jobs for which bar passage was required. Of

---

[*] Shareholder, Global Chairman of Professional Development & Integration, Vice President & Treasurer, Greenberg Traurig LLP.

[1] *See* NAT'L CTR. FOR EDUC. STATISTICS, https://nces.ed.gov/fastfacts/display.asp?id=372.

those 23,000, 16,000 took positions as lawyers in law firms employing at least two lawyers. Of those, there are roughly 3,500 positions at the largest 100 firms. Therefore, of the 3.1 million, you have already been whittled down to roughly 3,500. **You are one of the .1%. Relax. Enjoy!**

Well, perhaps the word "relax" isn't necessarily the best advice, but you should take a moment to appreciate all that you have accomplished. In this chapter, we are going to start preparing you for the wild ride that is being a junior associate. To be successful, you first have to understand the expectations of a typical first year in a large law firm. For that matter, you need to understand that nobody is typical and no two people will expect exactly the same thing. While one person may think you are doing just fine and experiencing the typical, steep learning curve, you may find a senior associate breathing down your neck, making you feel incompetent.

The simple truth is this: both are right. You may not feel terribly competent the first year of practice, but that is because you aren't necessarily taught in law school the most relevant, practical aspects of daily law practice. Law schools have made some significant changes in how and what they teach, but they remain confined to teaching to a Bar exam and according to an accreditation process. As a Vice-Chair of Vision 2016, a Florida law school effort to drive change in legal education, I have seen many law schools creating innovative, practical programs, but legal pedagogy still teaches you things you may never need in your daily practice. And you may not have learned some of the practical things we senior leaders in law firms are looking for from our associates. I have therefore been asked to be as practical as possible in helping you understand what people want from you.

Our expectations of junior associates can be boiled down into a few basic things:

Careful thought and analysis, excellent organizational skills, the ability to manage up (as well as down and across), the ability to learn from mistakes, and consistent quality on everything you touch are all expected. And in addition, an interest in and knowledge of cutting edge technology, great client relationships, and being a team player will be the icing on the cake. Only the first attribute listed here—careful thought and analysis—is something you probably studied in law school. The other factors are simply attributes you have probably demonstrated to come as far as you have. On the other hand, sometimes natural intelligence or even great organizational skills helps hide other deficits.

Let's walk through some examples of associates demonstrating they had what it takes to succeed.

Example One: Provide Careful Thought and Analysis

You are given your first research project on a matter you have never heard about. It involves something to do with the ability to sue for damages based on a very specialized law. You can't find anything on point in the case law. Nothing comes up regardless of whether you are doing key word searches or key note searches. You are close to giving up. But before you do that, think about where there are any kinds of analogies you can make to other laws or situations. One of the best legal research memos I saw came from an associate who came up empty on case law; however, she realized that she could argue the same legal theory based on seemingly different, unrelated cases she found. I asked the associate how she came up with that approach, and she said it was simply desperation. She found nothing, and she just needed to sit and think before she could face returning to me empty-handed. It worked. Her careful thinking yielded some useful approaches.

Example Two: Be Organized

An associate had to manage a multi-country structural reorganization. It involved creating, executing, and organizing multiple agreements for each of more than forty countries as a result of a new tax strategy. The first thing the associate did was prepare a chart that contained each country and what documents were needed for each one. That sounds simple enough, but what the associate did that took it up a notch was to insert links to the document in the document management system so that one person could open any document selected just by clicking on the link in the chart. It was genius, yet simple. I don't know that I would have thought to do that. But a combined knowledge of technology and how to leverage it made this person indispensable. Know how to manage your time, but also know what tools your firm has available. Know your resources and how to leverage them to benefit you and others. And if the partners and senior associates who supervise you don't know they exist or how to use them, take some time to tutor them on the new technologies. You will be making yourself indispensable.

Example Three: Be Able to Manage Up, Down, and Across

A partner will be the first to admit we don't always know everything we need to do in a given day. We try to stay focused on all the demands, but we also rely heavily upon our teams to deliver what we need, when we need it. Some of that means reminding us of deadlines and priorities, and other aspects include giving us work far enough in advance that you ensure we will have the time to review it in a careful, thoughtful way. Putting something on my chair at 7:00 p.m. when I have said it needs to go out first thing the following morning is probably not the best approach, unless I just gave it to you at 5:00 p.m. However, if I gave you something and say I need to deliver it to the client for review in a week, giving it to me in three days gives me the time and space I need to review it. And then when you remind me to send it out after another few days, you've again shown that you own the work as yours. We expect that you will take that ownership and be sure that everything you touch makes it to the finish line perfectly.

The reverse is also true. I expect you to be sure you have final approval before sending documents to the client or opposing counsel. If I say I don't have time to look at it before it goes out, that means I both trust and rely upon you for careful proofreading. You may want to take it upon yourself to find a colleague whom you trust to be your proofreader, but ultimately you are responsible for anything that might be incorrect—including anything your assistant reviews. If you have a great assistant, that's terrific, but even if he or she proofreads something for you, you are still responsible for any errors or typos. That means taking responsibility when things go wrong, and letting me know you alone are responsible. Again, mistakes do happen, but how you deal with them and take responsibility in the face of more senior attorneys is critical to building those important relationships.

And finally, your ability to be humble, kind, and respectful with everyone at your firm will be noticed. As a new attorney, you are walking into an office with receptionists, office services professionals, paralegals, and legal secretaries who may have been doing their jobs since well before you graduated from high school and possibly before you were even born. They have a lot of wisdom to offer and can make your job and life much easier. Do yourself a favor and respect their knowledge and experience because they deserve it and will be loyal to you if you treat them appropriately.

Example Four: Learn from Your Mistakes

I once had an associate call me to say he had made a mistake and inserted the wrong language in a settlement agreement. On the one hand, I appreciated his candor. But when I got a call a few months later with a confession of the same kind, it gave me pause. I know that mistakes happen, I truly do. But I expect a few things related to those mistakes: first, that you review your work carefully enough that you catch them before I do. It is one thing if you misunderstand an unclear direction once in a great while, but making a mistake or forgetting something cannot be something that repeats itself. When that happens, people learn from that—they learn they can't rely on you. And if an attorney can't rely on you, he or she won't give you more work. We start giving that work to other people who we trust and know we can rely on 100%. Is that a high standard? It certainly is, without question. But it is also one of the primary reasons why those numbers cited at the beginning of this chapter are so small. It takes a lot to get to this level. Our clients expect a tremendous amount from us, and they pay a very high rate to obtain that level of service, trust, knowledge, and reliability.

So, you need to track and learn from your mistakes. If you miscalculate a tax proration or a tenant fee per square foot, it may be that you simply didn't know how to do it in the first place. Perhaps it wasn't taught in law school and your partner or senior associate failed to show you how in detail. Perhaps you failed to ask. But once you learn how to do it, you need to be sure you have either a careful system or a great memory to be sure you can apply that knowledge the next time you face that situation. If, a month later, you have a similar assignment and again don't know how to do it or make the same mistake, you will be raising a red flag to those around you that you aren't picking things up quickly enough. Make a point of finding out the answer yourself, if necessary, but be resourceful to continue to learn and grow at all times. It may be easier to simply ask the assigning attorney who is next door, but it may be harmful to your reputation.

Example Five: Be Consistent on Quality

Consistency is about quality control. Assuming you learn from your mistakes, as you just read about, you will consistently improve your work quality by slowing down and taking the time to check your work carefully. The trick with this for a first year associate really relates to being a bit obsessive. It means checking your work over and over. It means taking a break, working on something else, and returning to it with a fresh eye. It also means reading things slowly and out loud. It means never relying on forms too much. If your brain turns off because you are using a form, that's when you are most likely to leave the last client's name in a form rather than revise it everywhere. Regardless of all the tools available to help you and all the assistants the firm provides, your name is on the document and there is no way to pass along responsibility to anyone else. So keep your brain on at all times. If you can't think anymore due to lack of sleep, take a break, get an extension, and do whatever else you need to do. Always reread that email before you hit send, even if you just made one minor change. You will be glad you did because your reputation for quality will grow from there.

Example Six: Know the Future of the Practice—Learn the Technology and Embrace It

If you are like me, you have a smart phone and a tablet, and you use them all the time. But I am hoping you are not like me in that you know more about what new technology is out there to help you be more efficient. As the newest generation in the workplace, the more senior attorneys are looking to you to keep us cutting edge. In fact, many law schools and organizations are targeting young attorneys to discover and help develop new technology in legal practice. I may be accustomed to assigning people to look for the words "orange juice" in thousands of emails in the discovery process, but I rely upon people like you to tell me, "Brad, I don't actually need to do that. There is software that we can train to look for the word in all the emails, and it will save the clients thousands of dollars." Partners expect you to stay up-to-date and be ahead of the curve. That means reading a lot, all the time. We expect you to read legal periodicals and stay up-to-date in your legal area, but we also expect you to be knowledgeable about the business world and trends. The associate that reads about artificial intelligence in the legal world and reads the *Wall Street Journal* on a daily basis will simply be further ahead than one who doesn't.

And it's not just new technology that we expect associates to master. Most senior lawyers expect associates to also be more adept with existing firm technology than anyone else. We expect our newest talent to know more than we do, so, for example, if we need calculations done for a closing, you should be able to use Excel's formulas and whatever else Excel can do without going to the Tech team for assistance. Again, we expect you to put in the extra time to make yourself indispensable because, ultimately, more and more of our clients see us as fungible. As external clients narrow the number of law firms they are using, we don't want to give them a reason to use another firm instead of ours.

Example Seven: Get to Know Our Clients

The best thing you can do is get to know the clients on whose matters you work. You may work with a few people that shield you from their clients, at least in the beginning, and it is good to know who those individuals are that don't want you to have client contact. However, if you are doing a good job, we want you to get to know our clients. You should be researching their companies and backgrounds and asking insightful questions about their challenges and goals, both on their own behalf and for the company. By doing that, you are meeting our expectations as someone who can handle the relationships as well as the work. That leaves us free to go focus on bringing in more work and more clients. More importantly, the client contact is more likely to pick up the phone and call you directly in the future. When you get integrated with our clients, you are showing your potential to build your career with us.

Example Eight: Be a Team Player

I'm sure you heard all about this in the interview or summer associate process, but it is true and can't be overstated: We expect you to work well with just about everything. You should respect our staff as part of the team, **and you should view no work as beneath you.** Instead, we expect an attitude of whatever is needed to get the job done. If you can work seamlessly with others, especially when large matters are split amongst several people, the work quality is generally more consistent and requires less management and revision.

Part of this approach to teamwork requires that you understand how difficult the first year or years of practice are. You may have to do some work that will make you think to yourself, "I didn't go through three years of law school for this." But actually, you did do just that. Doing routine legal work properly is a critical component to taking the next step in the practice of law. It needs to be completed accurately and on time. Performing basic work in the daily practice of law is what teaches you the judgment and process of a comprehensive practice.

Once you master the basic work, you can be trusted to perform more complex work; however, nuts and bolts of legal practice are important and never go away. Remember that even the most routine matter to you is extremely important to your client. If it is helpful, put yourself in the shoes of your clients and try to understand what is on the line for each of them. You may be ready for a larger role or more complex work, but if another case is important to the client and keeping you busy, that means the work needs to get done, and you are the selected person to do it. Patience is an inherent part of being a team player.

While there is a certain degree to which new associates are expected to "pay their dues," they also need time to develop essential skills and expertise. Many firms take a long view in developing associates, and associates should as well.

As you gain experience, however, if you are consistently a good performer and a team player, you will always be included on the best work.

Final Thoughts

I know you are thinking, wow, the expectations are high! And that is true; however, the payoff is tremendous challenge, growth, and satisfaction. For those of us who have been practicing law for decades, we can't imagine doing anything else. To be successful, you typically need to love what you do. If you don't love it, if the expectations are too much, don't be miserable. Talk to us. We more senior attorneys do have some wisdom to impart, and we didn't always love it from the beginning. Just as we expect you to work hard and be committed, it is fair to expect us to be committed to you and your development. If the people around you can help, let us know how. We are here to assist and challenge you at the same time. Remember, you are the future of our firms, and we are investing in you. We hope and expect you to take advantage of that!

Chapter 2

The First Six Months: How to Set the Right Tone

Jennifer L. Bluestein[*]

Your first year of practice is one of the most bewildering and stressful periods of your career; however, it is also the most thrilling and unique. You will look back on that first year and be amazed at just how much you have learned. This chapter will give you the best idea of how to be successful and introduces some of the topics covered in the remainder of this book.

Let's divide the advice in this chapter into four areas: gravitas, client service, work quality and efficiency, and accounting for your time. Some of these topics overlap, but everything is intertwined in the practice of law, so you might as well get used to that now. Your writing skills are always tied into efficiency, and your strategy always ties in

---

[*]   Global Director of Professional Development & Training, Greenberg Traurig LLP.

to your effectiveness. For that matter, your workload may impact your work quality (even though we hate to admit it). So facing the reality of how one thing impacts another is important.

Gravitas

Gravitas was one of the Roman virtues, referring to one's dignity or seriousness. In the modern world, gravitas is what causes a senior associate or partner (or even a client) to feel respect for and trust in you as a lawyer. For example, if as a 2L you went to your first Civil Procedure class and saw your new professor dressed as Bozo the Clown, you would probably have a hard time taking the professor seriously as an expert on Rule 23.

Be Mindful of Your Appearance

Your goal as a first year attorney is to instill confidence in others, and there are a few ways to do that. First, you need to look the part. That doesn't mean you have to ignore your uniqueness—it just means you need to consider your audience carefully. For example, if you work in an office where everyone wears jeans—even the newest, most junior people—chances are you won't be judged adversely for doing the same. But if you work in a place where most people wear suits on a daily basis, you don't want to stand out for wearing jeans and a t-shirt. I'm not going to tell you how to "dress for success" (that's an old book by an old Hollywood costume designer, Edith Head), but be thoughtful about representing the workplace and the firm. If you like to wear floral printed Doc Martens and extra wide bell bottoms, you should know that an outfit like that is going to raise some eyebrows, especially from some of the older partners who wear suits every day. For that matter, be aware that a department head who wears a suit every day is going to look more favorably upon a junior associate that comes in wearing a suit every day. Conversely, if you are in a practice group where everyone wears casual clothing, you will look a bit out of place dressing up every day. Of course, anything you wear due to religious observance should be absolutely acceptable in any workplace, and any office that gives you grief for that should have a human resources team to support and assist with any such situation.

You may benefit from some additional guidance on appearance. Do consider how you look as you enter the building, not just once you get to your desk. Don't wear flip-flops all summer long and change shoes at your desk because you will be riding the elevator with senior people looking down at your toes every day, judging you. Do make sure your hair is presentable each day (that includes facial hair). We have four generations in the workplace. Some generations view messy hair up in a ponytail as stylish, while others think it looks like a rats' nest. Make your own decisions, but again, read your audience. Don't think that everyone loves a long, messy beard (or, for that matter, that everyone appreciates the 5 o'clock shadow look that many young men are sporting). If you have a neat, trimmed beard, you may have one person who loves it and one who doesn't, but it isn't going to hurt an overall impression of you. In contrast, walking into work looking as though you forgot to shave, picked up a wrinkled, dirty shirt off the floor, and put on ripped shoes is definitely going to make several people think twice before entrusting you with their clients and billable work.

Law firms and legal agencies are trying to show they are more progressive and cutting edge than ever, which is true; however, at heart, attorneys tend to be more conservative and older than the general population. Once you have been at the job for a few months and convinced everyone you are the best new attorney they've ever seen, then you can think about how much you want to push the envelope and buck conformity. If you enjoy being different and risking some controversy, look however you want to look; just know you may have a tougher time instilling confidence. My advice: until you have wowed your employers and co-workers with your skills and professionalism, you are safer simply conforming to the typical office uniform.

Exude Self-Confidence

The other critical aspect of gravitas is how you hold yourself. We will cover communication a bit later, but also keep in mind that walking and talking with confidence that does not border on arrogance is helpful. You are there to learn and develop, not to show others that you know more than anyone else. At times you may feel like you are acting phony—either unduly subservient or falsely confident. That will pass. Being a new attorney in an office is like being the shiny, new penny in a drawer of pennies. You stick out of a crowd and everyone wants to see you when you are new. After the newness wears off, nobody pays much attention to you. Use it to your best advantage by creating an excellent first impression in every way.

Client Service

Meet and Beat Expectations

The second area of advice more seasoned attorneys will give you is to focus on incredible client service. Your clients are the other attorneys with whom you work, not just the outside clients you are serving. If a more senior attorney asks you for a draft of something, you want to be sure to treat that person as you would an external client. Your goal is to beat their deadline, deliver exactly what is expected, if not more, and to be accurate. A partner who tells you he needs to file a brief on Tuesday will not be happy if you deliver a draft on Monday night at 6 p.m. You may think that gives him twenty-four hours to review the document, but trust me, it isn't enough time. Instead, you need to ask the partner when you should turn in the draft, while reminding him you are a first year who hasn't written many briefs. Even if the partner says Monday is fine, beat the deadline. You will probably want to get the brief in the week prior so that he has a few days to review it and a couple of days to revise it or give you his edits.

Another effective method of client service relates to "managing up" or reminding the person for whom you are working of any potential roadblocks or time frames. In this example, you may want to remind the more senior attorney of a deadline or simply print out a document to save the supervising attorney the trouble of digging into her "inbox" for it. If you ask good questions, such as, "Do you prefer that I resend documents if I don't hear back within a day or two?," you will know how or whether someone wants to work with you.

Be Available, Proactive, and Responsive

Basic client service relies on excellent responsiveness. If you are given a smart phone on your first day on the job, it isn't so you can spend more time on Instagram. Instead, it communicates the expectation that you must always be reachable and responsive. Being an attorney is generally, unless you are told otherwise, a 24/7 job. While some large law firms have staffing managers who will schedule who is "on" or "off" on particular weekends, the general expectation is you will be checking your emails regularly, meaning possibly every hour during waking hours. And once people know you, they may be reaching out by text for an even faster response. What is expected? What is responsive? What is a fast response? That varies by employer and person, but it is something you should ask within your first few weeks and as you start any new matter or deal.

That said, everything is relative. If you are in the middle of a time-sensitive matter, every minute counts, so it may not be the best time to go to a four-hour movie and turn off your phone. On the other hand, you shouldn't feel like you can't hop in a hot, relaxing bath without your phone at your side when nothing urgent is going on at work. If you are a corporate attorney and you have a closing in two days, just sell your long-sought-after *Hamilton* tickets now. It isn't because "this is why you get the big bucks," although that is what some people may say. It is because being an attorney is a privilege. You are an officer of the court, a provider of services for those who do not know or understand the law the way we as attorneys do. In the same way a physician would not simply clock off shift at the stroke of 6 p.m. after she starts handling a new patient who comes into the ER, attorneys see things through and exhibit the professionalism at all times to know that someone can't always just step in and fill your shoes on a matter.

In terms of being proactive, this means you need to think ahead and anticipate what someone wants before the person even wants it. The best way to demonstrate proactivity is to provide updates or even possible next steps before the client (internal or external) asks. Show you are one step ahead and always thinking about the big picture. This level of proactivity will be appreciated, as long as you don't start the next project or facet until the client approves.

Understand Deliverables

In addition to understanding the level of responsiveness you need to demonstrate, you can stand out as exceptional by having frequent and effective communication skills, which is a key component of client service. I'm sure you have heard this old adage before: Never walk into anyone's office without a pen and paper in hand to take notes. But let's take that adage one step further. After you take an assignment and furiously write down everything you are hearing, wait thirty seconds to digest what you have heard. Repeat the assignment back to confirm your understanding, and ask the important questions. Try not to be so consumed with showing you are smart and competent that you feel you can't ask a few big picture questions. If it is billable work, you can always get that information from the attorney's legal assistant, but the big picture goal, the deliverable expected, and how that deliverable relates to the big picture is truly important. You can't provide great client service if you don't understand both the deliverable and the big picture. And if you feel too embarrassed to ask more questions, find out who else is working on it and could be a go-to for you (or at least someone who has experience with that kind of work).

Once you have that initial understanding of the deliverable, you should probably go get to work before you forget the nuances that you didn't capture in writing. If you procrastinate, you risk blowing your deadline simply because things always take longer for first years than more senior attorneys predict. One of the most important questions you should ask when you take an assignment is when you should get the assignment in and in what form (written, verbal update, etc.). And take note: when someone says, "Whenever you get around to it" or "Whenever you have a chance," do not believe that person for a minute. What the person is really saying is, "I don't need it on a specific day, but I'm testing you, so if you take more than a week, I'm going to wonder what's wrong with you." Of course, nobody will ever admit this and it probably isn't really the intent, but

I've heard time and time again either about a junior associate who completely forgot about an assignment or a partner who went looking for an assignment ten days later and was not happy to see the "deer-in-headlights look" of the junior associate who had not yet begun the task.

Manage Your Time

And finally, another important aspect of client service, which will be addressed in more detail in a later chapter, relates to time management. New attorneys' problems with time management usually arise in one of a few ways; the new attorney either: misses a deadline; refuses to take on an assignment but then has an unimpressive number of hours at the end of the month; or takes on new work and then gives it back incomplete or with poor quality because he or she simply "ran out of time." These are all mere setbacks, but if it becomes a pattern, even a pattern involving different assigning attorneys, people get concerned and start talking. Before you know it, you have earned yourself a reputation, and not one for which you are proud.

You will be told that if you can't meet a deadline or accept new work, you need to tell the assigning attorney something to the effect of, "I'd love to take that assignment for you, but I have X due on Friday and Y due on Tuesday. Is it possible that I could start working on this on Wednesday?" Or you will be told to say, "Ms. J has me working on this urgent project. Perhaps you can speak with her and determine which is a higher priority and let me know how to proceed." Those are both appropriate responses; however, there are some unspoken caveats to consider. Making a statement like either of those above and then showing 120 hours for the month in question will raise red flags to anyone who knows you had either of those conversations. More senior attorneys who see your hours will say, "Hmm, that associate really should have figured out a way to make it happen if their hours were this low." If you bill 180 hours or more that month, nobody will judge your making either of those statements. Overall, here is the caveat: if your hours are low, you should try to move heaven and earth to figure out a way to get both assignments done by their respective deadlines. This shows resilience, drive, and energy. Attorneys return to junior associates who always say, "yes," and always deliver.

Work Quality and Efficiency

And now we have saved the best for last, the most important thing to demonstrate in those early days: work quality and efficiency. If you have excellent work quality, everything else pales just a bit. You might be wearing a bozo costume, all wrinkled and disheveled, but if you are an amazing researcher, analyst, and writer, people will give you good reviews and maybe even admire your quirky nature. However, if you turn in sloppy work product at the beginning, your reputation will suffer and you will be fighting an uphill battle. Experienced attorneys expect new attorneys to lack experience or even basic legal knowledge, but they will expect new attorneys to demonstrate an eagerness to dig in and learn, as well as work product that is ready to be delivered to the client in the fundamentals: spelling, punctuation, grammar, and document formatting. An associate who turns in work that has even a few typos will not be trusted because the work will be seen as inconsistent.

Proofread Your Work

When it comes to typos, there are certain things you can pay attention to in order to avoid the typical pitfalls. First, don't simply rely on spellcheck. Run a proofreading program and be your own proofreader. Try to get your work done a day before it is needed in order to take time away and look at it with a fresh eye. Read it back page to front, reading it aloud if necessary. Take advantage of any technology available, such as Casetext's CARA or Contract Companion. Ask your technology and knowledge management departments, if you have them, whether those tools or the like are available to you. If your firm has a word processing department, ask if they perform proofreading as well. And finally, make a deal with the associate down the hall to carefully review one another's documents the first few months.

Always Think Carefully About What You Are Doing

The tougher aspect of work quality is careful thought about what you are doing. Based on your client service skills, you should have asked the right questions to understand the overarching goal for the matter on which you are working. Your challenge will be to keep that goal in mind while researching and drafting your work. If you are representing a buyer on a transaction, always think about whether the language you are using from a template or sample document would be used by the buyer. If it is language favorable to the seller, leave it out or ask your supervising attorney whether to add it in light of the party it favors. Also consider that a substantive change to one part of the document will likely change some other part of the document. After making minor changes, always do a final read through to look for those inconsistencies. And when you use templates, make sure every party name is accurate. I once sat in on a difficult review of a senior-level associate who had drafted a detailed memo to a client based on a prior one and failed to change the name of the client from the original memo. While that may appear to be a minor and easily fixable error, the attorneys overseeing that associate felt they had to review everything that went out from him before he hit send.

Learn to Properly Format Documents

Another relatively easy aspect of work quality is not even substantive, it is simply about how a document is formatted. Take the time as a new associate to do extensive training on Word and other MS Office Suite programs, if that's what your organization uses. You may be experienced with Google Docs, but if that's not what your new employer uses, you will invariably be less efficient. Take the time to understand how to use the formatting styles used at your firm. Some use the native styles in Word (assuming Word is used), while many others have overlays that are customized to the particular firm. Using tabs to make the document look right is probably the least efficient thing you can do. With less support staff allocated to attorneys, you are probably going to be doing the vast majority of word processing and document preparation yourself. If you learn the software and systems and apply them before you forget, you will be miles ahead of others who do not take the time to do so. Redlining, document cleaning, and cross-references are all standard tools attorneys need to know. If you aren't comfortable with all of that, you need to be. Again, this kind of skillset will help you be more efficient and set you apart at an early stage of your career.

Accounting for Your Time

As you begin your journey as an attorney, assuming you are in private practice billing your time, remember to account for all of your time. It is not your place to decide whether you spent too much time on something; that is your supervising attorney's role. It is simply your duty to accurately and ethically record the time. Anyone with experience knows it always takes longer than expected, especially for new attorneys. That is taken into account before the bills go out to clients. You need to keep others informed as to how much time you are spending and to be as efficient as possible with your time. Beyond that, it is for others to manage the bills. As long as you follow the advice above, you should have no problem becoming more and more efficient as time goes on. And if your work quality is increasing as you gain experience, you will receive more and more work. How you handle your schedule and workload as time goes on is a good problem to have, and one which we will explore in the next chapter.

Chapter 3

Taming Time for New Lawyers

Grover E. Cleveland[*]

The Challenges

Time management is a challenge for all lawyers, but it can be especially daunting for new lawyers.

Work does not come into law firms in a uniform stream. It may be helpful to think of large law firms like hospital emergency rooms. Firms are designed to handle urgent, complex matters on short notice. There are times you may worry about not being busy enough. A few weeks later when you are overwhelmed, you may long for the days when you were worried about how you would meet your hours. And it usually does not help to compare your workload to that of others in your class. At the end of the year, transactional

---

[*]   Attorney, Speaker, and Author, *Swimming Lessons for Baby Sharks: The Essential Guide to Thriving as a New Lawyer* (West Academic, 2d ed. 2016).

associates may be working around the clock, and litigation associates may be slow.

Early in your career at a firm, you may get many assignments from different lawyers. You may be the only one who knows how much work you have. And when you begin practice, you won't know how long projects will take.

Assigning lawyers should give you an estimate of how long a project will take. If you don't get an estimate, you need to ask. But if a lawyer is very senior, the lawyer may have forgotten the nuances involved in completing a polished product. An assigning lawyer may also assume that you know more than you do.

To add to the challenges, deadlines are usually firm: missing them is not an option. And circumstances can change on short notice. The project that was due "whenever" suddenly must be done by the end of the day. Or your calendar was clear, and then someone sought a temporary restraining order against a client.

To allay anxiety when you are slow, you may ask several lawyers for work. But there is often a lag between the time you indicate your availability and the time projects materialize. You can stay slow for what seems like an eternity. A few days later, everyone you contacted may need your help at the same time.

As if the vicissitudes of work were not enough, other factors such as procrastination can compound the challenges of completing many projects on time—every time.

Good time management habits can help you address many of these issues. But there are some important things to keep in mind. One of the most important is that it is *normal* to have slow periods followed by times you feel overwhelmed. Try not to add to your stress by imagining that either of those extremes will last forever. Use your slow times to recharge. Although you do need to pay attention to your hours, time off to recharge can help you handle the next deluge.

Remember that every other lawyer in the office has experienced time management challenges. Even with excellent time management skills, you are likely to feel overwhelmed at times. Don't panic, and don't be afraid to ask for help. One of the great advantages of working at a firm is that other people can help you—if you give them enough notice.

As you gain experience and build relationships with lawyers who become steady sources of work, you will find that it is easier to manage your time. You will be able to estimate how long projects will take, you will become more efficient, and you will be more likely to be pegged as a person who can help with any emergency.

Here are some time management skills to help you manage an often erratic work flow.

Plan Your Day

Start every day by planning your work. Constant planning is vital to help you tame time. You need to know what you have to finish that day, that week, and farther into the future. Then try to estimate how long you will need to complete the tasks over the next few days—and when you will do them. Also, set aside time to make progress on longer-term projects. That will help keep huge projects from sneaking up on you while you are focused on putting out other fires.

As part of the planning process, figure out what you may need from other people. Do you need information from another lawyer or the client? Will you need administrative support? Remember that other people need advance notice to plan *their* days so they can give you what you need.

Next, examine your projects to see if others could help on parts of them—even if you could do everything yourself. Could a paralegal start a document? Could a librarian identify some key cases? You are responsible for the work, but new lawyers often neglect to use all of the resources that firms provide. It takes time to stop and delegate, but ultimately, you are buying time for yourself.

Find Your Rhythm

Your planning will be more effective if you find your rhythm. That means doing the right work at the right time of day. Some people have the most energy and focus in the morning. Others are night owls. You should identify the times during the day when your energy and focus are at their peak. Many people are at the top of their game around 10 a.m. Energy may wane around noon and often increases again in the afternoon.

Try to do your most complex, critical work during the times of the day when you are at your best. This is the time when brilliant thoughts flow freely and you can provide the most value. Allocate less important tasks to other times of the day.

Also consider external factors when you plan. Many people are more productive at times when there may be fewer interruptions—typically, very early or very late in the day.

And working in blocks of time will make it easier for you to track your time and be more productive. Switching from one project to another can sap your focus and eat up time. On large projects, try to stay focused for a set period of time. Then you can take a short break, check your email, or shift to another project.

You will not always be able to do your most important work in uninterrupted blocks at the optimal time—but diligent planning will make it more likely.

Plan for Emergencies

Nothing upends careful planning like emergencies. Without warning, something obliterates your carefully structured day.

As you do your planning, block out some time for things you don't expect. You often won't know when an emergency will happen, but for most people, emergencies *will* happen. If you block out some time each day to handle minor contingencies, it is much easier to get back on track.

Another way to plan for emergencies is to give yourself a deadline to finish projects that is *before* the actual deadline. The deadline is not the only date you can finish a project; it is just the last possible date. And finishing a project early can help build goodwill for times you are cutting it close.

Your day may not go as planned. But having a plan will help ensure that you finish the most important work on time. And if you don't need the time that you set aside for emergencies, use it for a languishing project—or to get ahead on a long-term project.

Overcome the Overwhelming

Major emergencies may leave you feeling like you are drinking from a firehose. When you begin your career, you are likely to feel as if you don't know what you are doing. A huge amount of urgent work that you don't feel confident about can heighten your sense of disorientation.

Again, it is important to remember that most—if not all—lawyers have felt this way early in practice. And it gets better.

If you feel overwhelmed, one of the first things you need to do is take a time out. Breathe. Your goal is to focus on the work and not the swirl.

Double-check everything you have to get done to make sure nothing falls through the cracks. Just the process of making a list can reduce stress. The tasks become concrete. You can prioritize. And you will have a better idea of what you can do and where you may need help.

Check in with the assigning lawyer and work on a plan to make sure that everything gets done. You should not be afraid to ask for help. It's not a sign of weakness or failure. It is a sign of strength. And it is far better to ask for help than to blow a deadline—or cut corners. And of course, the more notice you can give people, the more likely they will be able to help.

Schedule Important, Non-Urgent Activities

Under the crush of deadlines, activities that are important but not urgent can languish. Examples include activities to expand your professional network or to enhance your substantive knowledge. You are more likely to complete the activities if you schedule them at the same time every day—preferably early in the day. Try to make at least some progress on these activities—even when you are stretched thin.

Know When to Set Boundaries

Sometimes a deluge of work comes from taking on too many projects. You need to be available to help other lawyers—particularly lawyers who provide you with regular work. If you tell lawyers you can't help with their work, they may not offer again. If a restaurant can't seat you, you go somewhere else, and you may not rush back. If a doctor can't see you when you are sick, you may switch doctors. You get the point.

But overpromising also causes problems. In trying to be helpful, it can be easy to say "yes" too quickly. You may find that you have agreed to a project without understanding the time commitment—or without considering the rest of your workload. If you take on too much, you may blow a deadline or sacrifice quality.

You may disappoint senior lawyers if you decline work. But the temporary disappointment is better than having to cut corners and getting a reputation for being sloppy. And if you screw up a project, you are likely to have to do it again—which will only compound your time management problems.

Because it can be hard to know how much work to take on, check with other associates in your group. They can help you understand what you can handle and what may be in the pipeline. Get in the habit of checking in with any lawyers who regularly give you work to find out how much of your time they may need in the coming weeks.

When things are busy, law firms will expect you to work longer hours to accommodate the demand. The firm can't tell a client that it can't do the work. Still, you may not be the right person for a given assignment.

If you need to decline new work, a soft "no" will help you maintain your relationships. Start by thanking the lawyer for thinking of you. Then explain your workload and propose a date in the future that you can help.

If you have a handle on your existing workload and you know what others have planned for you, you should be able to provide an accurate estimate. Your response could be something like this:

"I would love to work with you on this, but with my current workload, I would not be able to start until . . . ."

If you cannot provide an accurate estimate of when you could start the project, it is wise to avoid committing on the spot. Try to understand the scope of the project and the time commitment involved. Then indicate when you can let the lawyer know whether you can take on the project. Confirm your workload and follow up promptly.

If you decline a project or propose a start date that won't work for the assigning lawyer, you may get some pushback. The assigning attorney still needs someone to do the project. You can help your answer stick by suggesting one or two other associates who could assist.

Plan Your Projects

Planning your projects before you dive in is also critical for ensuring that you stay on track and use your time efficiently. Before you start a project, get detailed information about the work product, the client's goals, an example of the work product, and suggestions about the best way to start the project.

After you get an assignment, confirm precisely what the lawyer wants you to do. Repeating your understanding of the assignment may seem awkward, but it can clarify areas of potential confusion and highlight any unstated assumptions.

With surprising frequency, senior lawyers receive assignments that are not what they expect. And having to redo a massive project can crater careful planning. Senior lawyers often assume junior lawyers know more than they do, and junior lawyers are often reluctant to ask questions. That combination is a recipe for a project gone awry.

Organize the key tasks for a project before you start. Then decide how long they are likely to take. If you see any opportunities to delegate, do that right away.

When you have started on a project, check in immediately if you think you may be off track. And check in if the amount of time you have spent does not correspond to your progress. The assigning lawyer's estimate of the time required may not be realistic. But the estimate may relate to what the project is worth to the client. Checking in can help prevent surprises.

Curb Procrastination

Some projects are just unpleasant—or boring or daunting. For innumerable reasons, you can worsen your time management challenges by procrastinating. Unpleasant projects rarely go away. And letting them languish just makes them more difficult, time-consuming, and more painful. In the moment, it is easy to put them off. You can do them tomorrow and tomorrow. That feels like freedom. But soon you are in a bind.

Everyone procrastinates, and it won't help to beat yourself up. But you do have to start the work.

You are more likely to procrastinate when you think you have plenty of time: any consequences from not doing the project are far in the future. But the "reward" of delay is immediate.

It may help you to overcome procrastination to identify what is blocking you. Are you worried that a project is over your head? Does it seem boring? Are you worried that as soon as you complete the assignment, there will be others, and your life will involve work without end?

Sometimes the problem is procrastination itself. The next step that you need to take may reveal a lack of progress. For example, you may need to ask a question that will make it obvious to another lawyer that you have not started. So you delay the reckoning even more.

Identifying the cause will help you with the solution. And the solution is to start. For example, if you are dreading turning in a brief because you are worried you will receive negative feedback, question your assumptions. Then shift your focus to how you can meet the expectations.

Lawyers often put off tedious tasks, such as entering and releasing time. Of course, with delay, many tasks become even more tedious and time-consuming. You may be able to make tedious tasks more stimulating by making them harder.

Challenge yourself to do a tedious task thoroughly and completely in as little time as possible. How quickly can you enter and release your time from the day before? And for tasks that seem overwhelming and difficult, try breaking the task down into smaller and smaller tasks—until you have identified a few specific steps you can take that are absurdly simple. Those steps may even include delegating to others.

As part of your day-planning process, try to get into the habit of starting your day with an unpleasant task—first thing—at the same time every day. Mark Twain said, "If it's your job to eat a frog, it's best to do it first thing in the morning. And if it's your job to eat two frogs, it's best to eat the biggest one first." If you get in the habit of starting your day with an unpleasant task, you can usually look forward to having the day get better. Rewarding yourself after you eat your frog will help reinforce the habit. As an aside, releasing your time is an ideal frog.

Unpleasant projects may be easier to swallow if you promise yourself you will only take a small bite. Commit to starting and working for a short period of time. Set a timer for one or two billing increments. Start working, and then give yourself permission to stop when the time is up. Once you have started, you may have momentum and keep going. But even if you don't persist, you will have made some progress. And as you progress, the task may seem more palatable than you imagined.

Since the luxury of time makes it easier to procrastinate, focus on the ultimate consequences. Think about what will happen if you *never* do the project. Reframe your choice as either doing a task immediately—or never doing it and accepting the consequences. If this approach does not help you dive into a task, take another tack, because the project is not going to go away.

Finally, with small tasks, work on starting and finishing right away. If you can respond to an email the first time you read it, you won't have to flag it, find it again, read it again, and then respond.

Conclusion

Planning your day, "eating the frog," and other time management techniques won't eliminate the challenges of juggling multiple projects. But diligent time management will allow you to get more done with less stress and help you advance in your career.

Chapter 4

42 Ways to Work Inclusively in an Increasingly Diverse Workplace

Sandra Bang[*]

The topics of diversity and inclusion (D&I) have been discussed and efforts have been made to advance D&I goals in the legal industry for years. Law firms, legal departments, law schools, and other legal industry organizations have subject matter experts educating people on what it means to work in a diverse environment, how the organization can advance D&I goals, and how a more inclusive environment can be created and sustained—just to name a few examples. This is not surprising given that there are plenty of data-driven studies that show that diverse teams produce better

---

[*]   Chief Diversity & Talent Strategy Officer, Shearman & Sterling LLP.

financial results, and by increasing diversity, the probability of attaining breakthrough insights and solutions increases.[1] Let's face it: the question is no longer "what is the business case for diversity?" but rather, "what is the business case for homogeneity?"

Despite all of these discussions, studies, and efforts, the data seems to reflect that the legal industry has not moved the needle when it comes to D&I. Indeed, the American Bar Association's National Lawyer Population Survey[2] for 2018 shows 64% of active resident attorneys are male and 36% are female; since 2008, the numbers have changed less than 5%. The same study shows 85% of active resident attorneys identified as being Caucasian/white, 5% African-American,

---

1. David Rock & Heidi Grant, *Why Diverse Teams Are Smarter*, HARV. BUS. REV. (2016), https://hbr.org/2016/11/why-diverse-teams-are-smarter. Rock and Grant refer to the 2015 McKinsey report, *Diversity Matters* (Feb. 2, 2015), by Vivian Hunt, Dennis Layton, and Sara Prince, where Hunt, Layton, and Prince reviewed 366 public companies and found that those in the top quartile for ethnic and racial diversity in management were 35% more likely to have financial returns above their industry mean, and those in the top quartile for gender diversity were 15% more likely to have returns above the industry mean. Reference is also made to the Credit Suisse Research Institute July 2012 report (https://www.credit-suisse.com/corporate/en/media/news/articles/media-releases/2012/07/en/42035.html) outlining the global analysis of 2400 companies and finding that those that had at least one female board member yielded higher return on equity and higher net income growth than companies that did not have any women on the board. Rock and Grant themselves argue that diverse teams are smarter because they focus more on facts (being more likely to constantly reexamine facts and remain objective, and encouraging greater scrutiny of each team member's actions), they process those facts more carefully, and they are more innovative. *See also* Katherine W. Phillips, *How Diversity Makes Us Smarter*, SCI. AM. (2014), https://www.scientificamerican.com/article/how-diversity-makes-us-smarter/.

2. *See* https://www.americanbar.org/content/dam/aba/administrative/market_research/National_Lawyer_Population_Demographics_2008-2018.authcheckdam.pdf.

5% Hispanic, 3% Asian, 1% Other, 1% Native American, and 1% Multiracial. The ten-year trend shows that generally, there has been a less than 2% change in these numbers. Regarding leadership in law firms, the 2017 Report on Diversity published by the National Association for Law Placement indicates that women and minority partners are still under-represented at U.S. law firms. In 2017, women represented 22.7% of partners in major U.S. law firms, a small increase from 22.13% in 2016, and from 12.27% in 1993. Minority partners accounted for 8.42%, up from 8.05% in 2016 and 2.55% in 1993. Minority women made up 2.9% of partners at major U.S. law firms in 2017—thereby continuing to be the most dramatically under-represented group at the partnership level across all firm sizes and most jurisdictions.

Even if the ability to recruit diverse legal talent is strong, and diversity is successfully attained and retained, it is meaningless without inclusion. Diversity and inclusion are distinct concepts and both are essential to producing optimal business results. Verna Myers said it best: "Diversity is being invited to the party. Inclusion is being asked to dance."[3] In the work environment, diversity means representation. To achieve better results, innovations, and optimal outcomes, inclusion is a requirement. Without inclusion, the crucial connections that attract diverse talent, encourage their participation, foster innovation, and lead to business growth will not result.[4]

While leaders of your organization are ultimately responsible for setting the tone, policies, and standards, as an associate, you CAN contribute to creating and sustaining an

---

3. Verna Myers, Inclusion Strategist, https://vernamyers.com/#blogger.
4. Laura Sherbin & Ripa Rashid, *Diversity Doesn't Stick Without Inclusion*, HARV. BUS. REV. (Feb. 1, 2017).

inclusive work environment—not just for your benefit, but for the benefit of your teammates and the business of which you are a part.

Being respectful of differences and more inclusive in a diverse workforce takes effort. It will not always be easy. However, given the benefits of being more inclusive—better decisions made, increased engagement and collaboration, better results for clients, more satisfying environment where everyone has the opportunity to do their best work and be at the top of their game—isn't it worth the effort?

What can YOU do to work inclusively? How can you take action to help move the needle on D&I for your team and organization? Here are 42 ways and how to's:

1. Think about diversity and inclusion consciously and intentionally, using the suggestions in this chapter. Think about it when you do anything and everything. This will require effort and practice. You could set up a reminder, tickler, or checklist to help you be mindful about being more inclusive when taking action.

2. When you are asked to set up a meeting or gathering, ask yourself: Should anyone else be included? Could anyone else be included so that a greater variety of input is received? The final decision as to who is at the meeting may not be yours; however, you are being helpful to the organizer, and being inclusive, by asking the question.

3. Always ask: Are we working with real and true *facts*? Dig, do your diligence, and ask questions to get to the facts. Sometimes new associates may be afraid to ask questions for fear of appearing incompetent or inadequate. In actuality, you appear curious and engaged when you ask thoughtful questions.

4. Ask why. Asking why can help get to the facts or the root answer. This is particularly helpful when the initial response or answer appears superficial.

5. Never assume anything. Keep drilling down until you KNOW that something is fact rather than making an assumption about a person or a situation. Assumptions lead to misunderstandings and often the wrong answer, and they are often based upon bias.

6. Never presume. Presumptions can cause similar issues to those resulting from assumptive thinking. Ask questions to check your presumptions.

7. Take stock of your vocabulary and language. Can you use terminology that is non-gender-specific? More inclusive? Cliché language, for example, is often biased and does not encourage inclusive behavior. Doing research to use vocabulary that is accurate serves you and everyone else better.

8. Stop interrupting. Wait until the other person finishes speaking before you start talking. This indicates that you are practicing active listening.

9. Practice active listening. Active listening means to listen for understanding, not for preparing a response. It is important to actually think about what has been said to you, and even reflect on it, before you respond. Empathy also develops with understanding. Having a better understanding and empathy may enable you to provide a better response, and definitely a higher quality response than the one you may have given if you had interrupted.

10. Call attention to those who interrupt. This can be done in an appropriate and professional manner, and everyone in the meeting will appreciate it. For example, you could say to the interrupter: "Excuse me. Pat, hold that thought. Let's hear Chris finish what she was saying and then give our full attention to you and hear what you have to say. Thanks."

11. In a meeting, give every attendee an opportunity to express his or her views. You could even go "around the table" so that each person, without judgment, can share their thoughts or take a pass.

12. If you know someone in the meeting or group who may be an introvert and does not always speak up proactively, provide them a segue to contribute. You could say, "Taylor, what do you think about this topic? We would love to hear your views."

13. Interrupt bias. If you hear someone say something that you believe is biased, interrupt the bias by using humor or simply asking politely, "What makes you think that?" If you see something happening that shouldn't be happening—someone exercising poor judgment, making an inappropriate joke or state-ment—interrupt it. Question the statement and ask for clarification. You could also share how the joke made you feel, for example, or how the statement landed with the audience (e.g., uncomfortable, excluded, judged, offended, etc.). Questions can be asked in private, too, if helpful.

14. What and how are you labeling people; that is, do you think of certain types of people when you think of athletes, lawyers, overachievers, slackers, etc.? What are the ways in which you may be labeled? Think about how you do this, and how others do

this to you. Ask yourself if you can be inclusive as opposed to exclusive based upon the labels that you are placing on people.

15. Participate in reverse mentoring. Take advantage of an opportunity for you to reverse mentor someone who is not like you (i.e., different background, ethnicity, age, experience, ability, etc.).

16. At networking events within your firm, talk to someone outside of your practice group, office, or circle. Talk to someone you do not know. Expand your network. Learn something you do not yet know.

17. At conferences and other external networking events, introduce yourself to someone who appears to be different from you. Share something about yourself, and learn something new from someone you do not know.

18. Talk to the person who is alone at the networking event (could be about the weather just to get things started). He or she will likely welcome your approach. It may also be easier for you from a networking perspective since you would not have to break into a group.

19. Once you are no longer a "new associate" or "new employee" in your organization, reach out to the new person in your office, practice group, or department. Invite them to attend a program or event at your organization with you. Help them integrate and meet other people. Become a resource for them.

20. Continue getting educated. Participate in diversity and inclusion programs at your organization. Attend an inclusion network or affinity group event.

Spend time reading on a specific D&I-related topic that is of particular interest to you or about which you don't know very much.

21. Do you know your organization's diversity and inclusion strategy? How can you help and support the execution of that strategy? Get involved.

22. Join an inclusion network or affinity group in your organization. Get to know people and be a part of the forum in which relevant topics are discussed and support is provided.

23. Join an ally group. You may not be in a particular diverse category, but that does not mean you cannot be an ally and support the group's strategy and goals.

24. Participate in your firm's engagement survey. By giving feedback in this regard, you are helping your organization create better policies, programs, and ultimately an environment within which everyone can be more engaged and contribute fully. Without feedback, your firm may not have the information and context to make improvements—and how does that serve you as an employee?

25. Provide feedback and insights appropriately to partners and other firm leaders about your experiences, especially if you are diverse or different from the partner or firm leader. This can be done in an appropriate setting and with empathy. They will appreciate your insights and give you the opportunity to effect positive change.

26. Ask for feedback. Refuse to rely exclusively on your own thoughts and your inner circle. Ask those around you how you are making them feel in meetings, for

example. Do you appear to value difference? Is there something you are doing or saying—or not saying or doing—that you should or could be? Ask how you can be more inclusive.

27. Be flexible and adaptive. Are you doing the same old, same old? Are you truly open to new ideas? You may want to consider your habits and remove outdated ones. Consider making room for different inputs. This is easier said than done, especially for lawyers. However, by having this kind of mindset, you will increase the probability of letting in and coming up with innovative recommendations and solutions for clients and yourself.

28. Increase your self-awareness. Do you know your communication style? Preferences? Have you taken the Harvard IAT implicit bias test online? What are your biases and shortcuts? Are there biases that you have, or assumptions that you make based on where someone went to law school, or their parental status, background, etc.? We all have blind spots. According to Eric Kandel, a neuroscientist at Columbia University who received a Nobel Prize for his work on memory, the mind works unconsciously. He estimated 80–90% of the brain works unconsciously. Regardless of the actual percentage, the reality is that experts agree that the ability to have conscious access to our minds is quite low. Therefore, we should actively work on combating our blind spots and examine and reflect on the shortcuts we may have in place regarding the way we think. Being more self-aware of both your strengths, weaknesses, and shortcuts will help you act more inclusively and welcome difference—and leverage both to your and your organization's advantage. One

practical suggestion is to consider using an image as a screensaver on your computer that can help you disrupt your bias. This is called counter-stereotyping imagery and can help you combat "mindbugs" (e.g., having shortcuts such as thinking short and bald men are senior executives, construction workers are men and wear hard hats, people pushing a baby stroller are women). Images can be found in Google, for example, and many advertisers have also been using counter-stereotypical imagery.

29. Expand your sources of news and social media. Get a variety of perspectives and inputs. It will help you think more inclusively and inject different ways of thinking.

30. Do one thing that makes you feel uncomfortable. Tolerate that feeling. Perceived safety in surrounding oneself with sameness—which avoids the potential conflict of acknowledging other perspectives—is a slippery slope.

Here are more ways you can be inclusive as you become more senior, take on managerial responsibilities, and have a stronger leadership role (albeit you may have opportunities to do the following even as a junior associate):

31. Be a model and demonstrate being inclusive by talking about diversity and inclusion openly and repeatedly. Talking about it signals that diversity and inclusion are important to you and the organization.

32. Be a model and demonstrate being inclusive by taking action to demonstrate your inclusive management and leadership skills. Characteristics of being an inclusive leader include: giving actionable

feedback, making risk-taking safe by creating a "safe environment" for others, taking advice and implementing feedback, empowering team members to make decisions, sharing credit for team successes, and ensuring everyone gets heard (see Center for Talent Innovation resources on their website for more information on this topic). Be mindful of how you run meetings. For example, switch up who runs meetings, as appropriate. By having different people lead meetings, there is a greater likelihood that different approaches to discussing topics, different group dynamics, greater variety of solutions, etc., will occur. This may be particularly helpful for regularly occurring meetings, which can become stale. Also, conduct meetings in a way where all attendees understand and believe that different approaches are welcome and everyone's point of view will be heard. Don't forget about the people who may be participating remotely. Make time and pause to allow those who are on the phone or on videoconference to have their say. Be proactive and make them feel like they are a part of the conversation. Also, if a program or meeting is happening in a large room, consider using microphones. Not everyone has the same hearing abilities and some people may be limited from participating if they cannot fully hear what is being said. Consider holding meetings or programs on different days and not just in the morning or evening. Holding events at the same time/date may exclude certain people from participating.

33. Can the systems and processes that you use or are a part of be more inclusive? Can they be revised, for example, to "automize" the inclusion of someone

or something different from the usual, rather than relying upon someone remembering to be more inclusive?

34. If you have an opportunity to pick the members of a team or group, ask yourself whether you are turning to your "usual" to fill your team. Consider those outside your usual group and add people to your team who are from a different department, generation, discipline, etc., as appropriate. You are increasing the probability of the group being more creative and thinking outside the box—and thus being more innovative.

35. Introduce people to each other—be a connector. Offering introductions between people who do not know each other helps others potentially solve issues they may be grappling with and most definitely expands their networks and sources for ideas and resources. Connecting people also indicates to others that you are thinking about how to help them and support their success.

36. Consider how you allocate work and staff matters. Can you be doing it differently? Can you be providing learning and development opportunities more expansively? Have you considered working with someone you haven't worked with previously? For example, can you help someone obtain a "stretch assignment" or gain exposure to a matter or skillset that she or he has wanted to develop, by staffing differently? Is there an opportunity for you to make an introduction or connection that impacts the way work is allocated and provides someone with an opportunity?

37. Ask yourself if you silence people, that is, make them feel like they cannot express themselves or act freely. It may be something you are saying—or doing. By being a "chilling effect," you may not be getting all the contributions and insights that you can be receiving, and thereby may be limiting the solutions that you are considering.

38. Think beyond the usual recommendations that you are making. Is there something you can do to think differently about potential solutions "outside the box" and before you make the final recommendation(s) to your client?

39. Consider other resources you can tap and get different or even unusual recommendations. Why not? This may help you get to a more innovative solution.

40. Mentor someone who is different from you. They could be someone who is of a different gender, background, skill set, age, experience, etc. You will likely learn something from the relationship too.

41. Give credit to those who actually come up with the idea. Sometimes ideas are summarized or repeated by others, and it is the last person to articulate the thought who receives the credit. If you see this happening, speak up, and attribute the contribution to the original person.

42. Change your context. Work in a different environment to get a different perspective. This could be as simple as sitting at a different angle to change the view in front of you, or working in a different part of your office or with different people around you. Changing your work environment can help you (lit-

erally) approach topics from a different perspective, ultimately facilitating the generation of different ideas and solutions.

Chapter 5

Practicing in a Global Environment

Olivia Tyrrell, Aria Eckersley,
Elizabeth Roque, and Josephine Bae*

Introduction

As businesses expand globally, law firms continue to need to meet their clients' needs. Firms that do not already have a large global presence may open offices outside of the United States or may engage other law firms in foreign countries to assist with its matters where the law firm does not have an office. If you work for an international law firm, you will be working across multiple jurisdictions with different attorneys around the world. Working for an international law firm or with international clients provides certain rewards and challenges. As a first year associate, you play an

---

*   Olivia Tyrrell is a partner at Baker McKenzie. Aria Eckersley, Elizabeth Roque, and Josephine Bae are associates at Baker McKenzie.

important role in your team and oftentimes will be communicating with local counsel frequently throughout your day and serving as the initial point of contact for your projects. In this chapter, you will learn about the cultural considerations, project management tips, as well as the changing international tax and business landscape to help you succeed as a first year associate in a global practice.

Cultural Considerations and Building Relationships Across Borders

As a first year associate, you will be tasked with communicating with lawyers across the globe for anything from requesting their assistance or local expertise for projects to scheduling meetings. This section will provide an overview of the cultural considerations you should take when working with local counsel as well as tips to build relationships across borders.

Email Etiquette and "Mirroring"

As you know, email communication etiquette is very important in today's technological world. When working across borders, there are certain cultural considerations you should be aware of in addition to the general communication etiquette you have been instructed on previously (checking for spelling, attaching any documents you reference, etc.). When emailing with your colleagues internationally, a helpful communication technique is to "mirror" the email etiquette your colleague uses. In some jurisdictions (e.g., European countries), email correspondence is typically more formal than the email correspondence you may use with other parties in the United States. For example, you may find that after working with counsel in London for a month, your colleague may still address every email to you with "Dear." If this is the case, the best practice is to mirror this same language in your responses. Similarly, if local counsel addresses emails with "Hi," it is appropriate to mirror this address in your response if you are comfortable doing so.

Although it may seem obvious, when emailing with local counsel, be sure to double check that you are spelling your colleague's name correctly as spell check may not capture a large variety of names. If your colleague's name includes any hyphens or accents, you should be mindful of this spelling and address them in email as they spell their name in their email signature.

Schedule Sensitivity

When working across borders, you should be conscious of the schedules and holidays of international counsel. Although not necessarily true everywhere outside the United States, it is important to be sensitive to the fact that different jurisdictions approach working on holidays and weekends differently. Although it is not appropriate to make generalizations about what a work week looks like in another jurisdiction, you should aim to be sensitive to other jurisdictions' schedules and holidays, recognizing that law firms in the United States may have a different approach. That said, as service providers, our role as lawyers is to understand and meet client expectations. Local counsel are a part of the overall team. Hence, it is important to communicate with local counsel as soon as possible the timing expectations, particularly if this will require them to work on holidays or over weekends.

As a first year associate, you may be responsible for setting deadlines for local counsel in a project. When setting deadlines, you should always: (i) consider the difference in time zones and (ii) set deadlines that permit sufficient time for you to review the work product provided by local counsel, ask follow-up questions, and collate all responses to present a work product that is consistent and reads as though written by one author, but at the same time provides local counsel with sufficient time to prepare their input. For example, if you would like to begin reviewing local counsel's work product first thing Monday morning, setting a Monday close of business deadline local time typically works out well. This allows local counsel the flexibility to determine how to allocate their time if they prefer to work over the weekend or to work on the project during the course of their day on Monday. As discussed later in this chapter, considering time zones is crucial to working across borders.

Practice Tip: If you are staffed on projects with multiple jurisdictions, print out an online monthly calendar and add the holidays that your jurisdictions' offices will be closed. If your law firm has international offices, the firm's website may include notices about office closures in its different locations. For example, on the Baker McKenzie internal home page, the top of the page includes upcoming office closures around the world as well as a digital calendar including these closures. As a first year associate, you are responsible for knowing the details of the project and these schedule considerations are no exception.

Building Relationships

In law firms, you will often hear that you should treat everyone like a client. That is, you should give other associates, partners, and specialists the same respect and deliver them the same high-quality work that you would provide to a client. International counsel should be included in this "client" list as well. Delivering high-quality work product, drafting thoughtful emails, and fostering your relationships with local counsel is just as important to succeeding as a first year as following these practices with your domestic colleagues.

When working with counsel across borders, you are acting as a representative of your firm and you should be mindful of this fact whenever you are communicating with international counsel. Many times you will find that you will work with the same people or group of people from international offices on a number of projects. As a representative of your firm, you should always strive to meet deadlines, communicate effectively, and be courteous with counsel. You should also keep in mind that these people may someday be work providers to you!

In general, the email etiquette and schedule sensitivity outlined above are critical components of building relationships with local counsel. Demonstrating respect and sensitivity to counsel will help to build trust in your relationship and lead to a more successful partnership. An important key to building relationships with counsel is to add a more personal approach to your communication, while maintaining appropriate boundaries. At times, it may be easiest to pick up the phone or send an instant message to another local counsel associate. This can break down the formal barriers and help to create a more comfortable relationship where you can easily reach out to local counsel with questions, and vice versa. Creating this open line of communication demonstrates that you are available to local counsel and builds trust.

Practice Tip: Use your firm's resources whenever you have questions. If you are ever uncertain about communicating effectively with colleagues across borders, there are many resources for you to turn to. A great first place to begin is in the online or written resources your firm may provide. For example, Baker McKenzie offers a mobile application to help attorneys understand the differences in communication styles internationally. In addition to online resources, you should feel free to reach out to other colleagues in your office with experience with a particular office or in a certain jurisdiction who may be more familiar with the issues you face. Issues you might ask your colleague about include:

(i)   the international office's preferred method of communication and level of formality (email, phone calls, or instant messaging);

(ii) effective ways to communicate deadlines with local counsel; and

(iii) your colleague's experience with an office's working schedules (late nights, weekends, or holidays).

It is important to note that any advice or information you receive about a particular jurisdiction or international office may not apply across the board to every attorney or every law firm. However, gathering information in order to be aware of potential cultural differences will help you to be a more collaborative and better-equipped lawyer—which will pay rewards as you become more senior in light of the ever-increasing need for teamwork.

Cross-Border Project Management

Coordination, organization, and project management are key skills to develop as a first year at an international law firm. You will be required to keep track of a number of legal issues from jurisdictions across the world, and to ensure that those issues are addressed and resolved at the proper time. The following sections discuss practical considerations for coordinating global projects and ways to prepare for and understand the nuances you will encounter during your first cross-border transactions and projects.

Coordinating Global Teams

As a first year, your role on international deals will involve a lot of coordination. Often, you will be the main point of contact to your colleagues around the world, and it is important to stay organized and conscious of the many moving parts of a given project. For example, on any given deal, you may find yourself working with colleagues from different functional groups (employment, benefits, real estate, finance, etc.) in the United States, as well as colleagues and correspondent counsel from different jurisdictions.

Do your best to manage expectations (both yours and your counterpart's) for the duration of the project. If you anticipate needing extra time to review documents or comments from colleagues where the laws are substantially different from the U.S. laws you are familiar with, try to provide enough lead time for you and your colleagues to collaborate to produce a clear, understandable product. Moreover, be sure to respond to any questions in a timely manner and ask prompt follow-up questions to your international counterparts while the issues are still fresh. For example, on a multi-jurisdictional deal, it can be helpful to address outstanding issues with your colleagues in Europe first thing in the morning, while the European workday is ongoing. Your questions for colleagues in Asia can be addressed later in the day so that they are addressed first thing in the morning in Asia, which gives you time in the evening to discuss any follow-up items.

From a practical perspective, it is not always possible to ask questions or discuss issues at the optimal time of day. However, if you keep time zones in mind and consider the needs of your colleagues to get the work done, you will make everyone's life easier as you coordinate on a global basis.

Using Organizational Resources to Prepare

One thing to remember as a first year associate is that your firm likely has a vast number of resources to help you succeed during a cross-border project. Although it happens, it is rare at an international law firm that none of your colleagues have ever encountered the issue you are facing with another jurisdiction. Don't be afraid to ask associates, paralegals, project managers, librarians, and other specialists (or even partners!) at your firm if they are familiar with the problem or can point you in the right direction. Many times, what seems like a unique or perplexing local law issue is run-of-the-mill for your colleagues who come across these issues on a daily basis. Before long, you will be a resource to the next incoming associate.

Keep in mind that in addition to your colleagues, your firm may have helpful precedent and background material from which you can learn about a particular project or international work as a whole. For example, Baker McKenzie has developed a cross-border M&A heat map that gives an overview of the complexities and challenges of completing cross-border transactions in forty-nine countries across the world and has many multi-jurisdictional surveys of a variety of issues, which may already address what you are looking for and enable you to produce a work product for the client at a much lower cost. If you invest time in learning about the baseline considerations of cross-border work up front, you will be better situated to coordinate and manage your projects and their unique complexities later on.

Using Technology in a Global Environment

Today's technology allows you to communicate with people around the globe in a matter of seconds. As a first year, you can use technology to your advantage in choosing the best time and method of communication to ensure prompt resolution of any issues. This section will discuss the things to keep in mind when interacting with colleagues and counsel around the world.

Email, Instant Messaging, and Phone Use: Situational Pros and Cons

There are myriad options for getting in touch with your colleagues and counsel outside the United States. While email and telephone are historically the most straightforward ways to communicate, many firms have implemented firm-wide instant messaging that can greatly increase the speed at which you resolve minor issues or get clarification from your counterparts around the world. While all of these communication methods have their own benefits and drawbacks, it is important to take certain considerations into account when choosing how best to get in touch with someone.

For example, not all offices or firms will use instant messaging in the same way—and there may be cultural differences in how casual IM communication is. You also want to take into consideration potential language barriers (it may be easier to type out lengthy legal analysis rather than to discuss it live or via instant messenger) and the time of day (your colleagues may be out of the office for the day but responsive to email). Choosing the proper method of communication can be critical to resolving issues in an efficient and convenient way.

Managing Time Zones with Technology

Working with colleagues and counsel around the world presents the unique challenge of juggling multiple workdays. In order to keep the project on track, you should consider when your global counterparts will be available and responsive to your questions and requests. For example, by the time the Friday workday begins across the United States, much of Europe and Asia have begun their respective weekends. If you need something to be completed by Monday morning, it is important that you communicate with your global colleagues as soon as practicable to ensure they have enough lead time to respond to your request.

There are a number of ways you can use technology to plan around the many time zone differences that you might be working with. For example, the World Clock Meeting Planner on timeanddate.com allows you to look at the time differences across jurisdictions and schedule a meeting at the most convenient time for all parties involved. This tool (and others like it) is particularly helpful to double check your work even as you gain familiarity with different time zones; for example, not all jurisdictions start and end their daylight savings time on the same date as we do in the United States (and some do not observe it at all).

Practice Tip: One simple way to effectively manage time zones is with clear, written communication. You can avoid confusion by clearly stating in your emails the time zone you are referring to with respect to meetings or deadlines. Likewise, if you are uncertain which time zone someone else is referring to, you should always ask up front to prevent misunderstandings.

Thinking Forward: Awareness on Recent Developments

As a first year associate, it is helpful to understand the big picture of the transactions or cases you work on. You should keep apprised of news, read internal or client alerts, and be generally aware of changes in the business and legal fields beyond your specialty. Of course, you will have to defer to specialists when it is necessary to do a deeper analysis, but you will be more successful and add value to your team if you are aware of issues globally—especially as they relate to your clients. For example, at the time of the writing of this book, significant wide-reaching developments included:

- **U.S. Tax Reform:** The enactment of major tax legislation at the end of 2017 called the Tax Cuts and Jobs Act is driving the behavior of both individuals and businesses and encouraging them to analyze what impacts the tax reform will have on them. The key changes include the permanent reduction in the corporate income tax rate and one-time repatriation tax.[1]

- **General Data Protection Regulation (GDPR)**: In 2018, the European Union enacted the GDPR in order to harmonize data protection obligations across the European Union. This regulation subjects companies to enhanced obligations with respect to their handling of personal data. In the M&A space, the GDPR will affect a wide array of areas, including what companies will look for during due diligence, how virtual data rooms are managed, and when sensitive information can be transferred.[2]

- **CFIUS**: The Committee on Foreign Investment in the United States (CFIUS) is a government agency that reviews national security considerations related to foreign investments in U.S. companies. In 2017, the CFIUS impacted a number of deals through tightened investment restrictions and export controls. As personal data concerns and technology continue to grow increasingly important, the CFIUS' impact on deal activity in various sectors such as Health and Biotech will continue to grow.[3]

Final Thoughts

It is an exciting time to be joining the legal field and working with colleagues and clients across the globe. There

---

1. Baker McKenzie, Tax Cuts and Jobs Act (2018).
2. Baker McKenzie, The Impact of the EU's New General Data Protection Regulation (GDPR) on M&A (2018).
3. Baker McKenzie, Rising Tension: Assessing China's FDI Drop in Europe and North America (2018).

are numerous resources and technologies to help you be a successful, effective, and efficient first year associate. From understanding cultural differences and managing large teams across borders, to keeping up to date with the latest changes in the business and tax landscapes, being a first year associate at an international law firm is challenging and incredibly rewarding. With the tools and tips outlined in this chapter, the resources offered by your firm, and the talented staff and attorneys at your law firm, you are well equipped to handle these challenges and start your legal career on the right foot. Good luck!

Chapter 6

Creating Positive Visibility

Jane DiRenzo Pigott[*]

What Is Positive Visibility?

As a first year associate, positive visibility is the combination of having people know who you are *and* having an instant positive view of you. When you think about creating positive visibility over the course of your career, you will think about it in terms of both inside and outside your organization. In addition, both internally and externally, you will want to create a form of positive visibility known as gravitas. As a first year associate, however, focus solely on inside the firm. Your "clients" are very likely going to be more senior associates and partners. Your "job" as a first year associate is to figure out the culture and politics of your group or team and to become a proficient substantive lawyer. Save the task of creating external positive visibility for next year.

---

[*]   Managing Director, R3 Group LLC.

Why Do You Want to Be Strategic in Creating Positive Visibility?

Creating positive visibility is not a tactical project. Be strategic about how you create a view of yourself among those who are more senior than you at the firm. Why do you want to invest in this activity? Senior associates and partners pick the newest members of their teams early and once teams are established, breaking into them can be very difficult. Many new associates are staffed on matters based solely upon their "reputation": "I've heard good things about . . . [on the partner/senior associate grapevine]." When you have a positive reputation, you increase your access to skill-building assignments and opportunities to create social capital with the "right" senior attorneys. In addition, positive visibility creates an opportunity for you to be top of mind or at least make the list of people considered for firm citizenship roles, which facilitates your visibility with attorneys with whom you may never have an opportunity to do a substantive project.

What Does Positive Visibility Look Like As a First Year Associate?

There are many ways to create positive visibility from the start. Here are a few ideas for you to consider and implement immediately:

1. Lawyers "sell" judgment. Whether you like it or not, how you dress impacts other people's impression of your judgment. Look around you at the firm. Until you have established standing through superior performance, "fit in" by dressing in a way that is consistent with those more senior than you in your group or on your team.

2. Come to meetings prepared. Ask another associate who has experience with the team or working with the partner about the "rules" for participating in meetings so that you can participate in a manner that will be viewed as appropriate. Participate in the pre-meeting banter—it helps create the impression that you communicate in a manner that enhances relationships. Only use your electronics if others are doing so.

3. Do some due diligence on the members of the team and the client. Every team has its own dynamic, and understanding the culture and politics of the team will help you create a positive impression.

4. Seek constructive feedback at the first appropriate interval. Ask the person who is immediately supervising you to provide an indication of what you are doing well and what you could do differently to be more effective. Implement the feedback and express gratitude for the non-billable minutes that were invested in you.

5. Seek out informal mentoring opportunities both with those with whom you are working and those who are "like" you, however you define that concept. If your firm has a formal mentoring program, invest the time in being very proactive in establishing a relationship with the mentor you are assigned.

6. Say yes to opportunities that are offered to you to create social capital. Accept the invitations to go to lunch, have a beer, drive a partner to a meeting, etc.

7. Begin to have conversations with more senior associates about what the appropriate skill set benchmarks are for your practice area. You need to under-

stand what substantive skills are necessary for you to be valuable to the clients (most of whom will be internal as a first year) and to be on track to matriculate. It is up to you to create a plan to seek out the "right" skill-building assignments. That action will be seen by others as you "taking ownership" of your career.

8. Use non-billable time to observe more senior lawyers "in action" on substantive matters, in client relationship activities, in business development, and in the activities they do to create external positive visibility and gravitas. Take full advantage of any programs supported by the firm for modeling opportunities.

9. Raise your hand and volunteer. Doing so will be seen as "taking initiative." Approach such opportunities with the same rigor that you would a billable project: do a high-quality, timely job on the project.

10. Work in the office, instead of remotely. Until you have established a solid reputation, it is important for people to see your face and be able to walk into your office and ask a question or give you an assignment.

11. Model your in-office work hours on those worked by more senior members of the team. You have to earn standing before you can work when and where it is most convenient for you. Do not underestimate the judgments that will be made if, for example, you do not get into the office until 10 a.m., even if you turn every assignment in on time.

12. Turn assignments in early, not just on time. Do things as soon as you get them. Create a reputation for saying yes and being responsive.

13. Provide updates to those with whom you are working that are short, punchy, and positive. If you get an assignment that is taking longer than expected, check in with the attorney supervising you. One of the worst things you can do as a first year is earn the reputation as someone who "shocks" with the number of hours billed on an assignment.

14. Go to firm social events. Talk to people you do not know, as opposed to hanging out with your friends. While it is fine to have a drink, do not get drunk or create a reputation that you are a heavy drinker. Only eat food that allows you to do so without wearing it.

15. Meet the others who work on your floor. It is your responsibility to go to their offices and introduce yourself. Make this effort as soon as you arrive.

16. Make a point of dropping by the offices of those attorneys with whom you are working. Do not remain a faceless name on an email distribution list.

17. Do not verbally abuse support staff. Be polite and civil to everyone, not just the lawyers.

18. Take advantage of training opportunities provided by your practice group and the firm. Even though these are non-billable activities, they will be high-value opportunities to enhance your skill set early.

19. Make sure you remain on pace to meet/exceed your billable hour target. If you are not on pace, seek more work early and often until you have solved this

problem. People will assume that you have a "quality" issue if you are not as busy as your peers.

20. Smile and greet people when you see them in the hall or on the elevator. As a new person, you have the opportunity to establish a reputation and you would be surprised how far a "hello" will get you.

When Do You Focus on Creating Positive Visibility?

You should start thinking strategically about creating positive visibility before your first day at the firm. Being a first year associate is overwhelming because there is so much to learn. Walk into your new role with a clear idea of what you will do to create positive visibility so that you are ready to integrate these ideas into what is sure to be a hectic first few months.

Chapter 7

The Importance of Pro Bono Legal Service

Julie E. LaEace[*]

> "Those who are happiest are those who do the most for others."
>
> **—Booker T. Washington**

When you first start practicing as a lawyer, your employer may or may not emphasize that you should get involved in pro bono work right away. Many large law firms have well-established pro bono programs with one or more individuals who run that program on a full-time basis. Smaller firms and other employers may not have established programs. Whether your new employer actively encourages it or not, unless you are in a particular position where you are

---

[*] Pro Bono Counsel and Firmwide Director of Pro Bono, Kirkland & Ellis.

prohibited from doing pro bono work (say, you are clerking for a judge, or have been hired by a government office that does not permit their attorneys to engage in pro bono legal service), as a new attorney you should consider how to incorporate some pro bono work into your practice from the get-go. In this chapter, we'll discuss why that is, and ways to get involved.

What Is It, and Why Do Firms Do It?

First, what is pro bono legal work? You may be well versed in the concept of pro bono legal service through your law school experience. Your employer may have a policy that defines pro bono differently, but the Pro Bono Institute, a national nonprofit that is mandated to explore and identify new approaches to pro bono legal assistance for the poor and disadvantaged, defines pro bono as legal work that is done without expectation of a fee for

> persons of limited means or to charitable, religious, civic, community, governmental and educational organizations in matters which are designed primarily to address the needs of persons of limited means; . . . individuals, groups, or organizations seeking to secure or protect civil rights, civil liberties or public rights; and . . . charitable, religious, civic, community, governmental or educational organizations in matters in furtherance of their organizational purposes, where the payment of standard legal fees would significantly deplete the organization's economic resources or would be otherwise inappropriate.[1]

---

1. Pro Bono Institute, LAW FIRM PRO BONO PROJECT CHALLENGE®, http://www.probonoinst.org/wpps/wp-content/uploads/Law-Firm-Challenge-2016-1.pdf (accessed June 12, 2017).

Pro bono legal work takes many forms: volunteering at a legal advice desk, assisting a low-income entrepreneur in setting up a small business, representing an individual fleeing persecution in his home country in asylum proceedings, or helping a small nonprofit obtain 501(c)(3) status are all examples of common pro bono projects.

Many large law firms have incredibly robust pro bono practices, donating thousands of hours of free legal service each year. In 2017, Kirkland & Ellis attorneys contributed over 126,000 hours of pro bono work. But why do law firms give away millions of dollars of free legal work each year?

Ethically Required

Every lawyer has a professional responsibility to provide pro bono legal services to those unable to pay. Many states have adopted some variation of ABA Model Rule of Professional Conduct 6.1. This model rule encourages lawyers to contribute at least fifty hours of pro bono service a year.[2] In 2012, New York implemented a requirement for bar applicants to complete fifty hours of pro bono service prior to admission.

Marketplace Expectations

More and more law schools are emphasizing the importance of pro bono as part of the law school curriculum. Some law schools, like Harvard, actually require J.D. students to contribute at least fifty hours of pro bono legal work as a condition for graduation. Law students graduating today

---

2. American Bar Association, MODEL RULES OF PROFESSIONAL CONDUCT r. 6.1 (2016), https://www.americanbar.org/groups/probono_public_service/policy/aba_model_rule_6_1.html (accessed June 12, 2017).

are now, more than ever, inclined toward volunteerism and giving back, and skill development is a driving factor.[3] To meet these expectations and remain competitive in attracting top talent, law firms have focused on building strong pro bono programs.

Legal departments of many corporations are also starting to focus to a greater degree on pro bono legal work. For a variety of reasons, they often look to partner on pro bono projects with the law firms that do the most work for them.

Finally, law firms and individual lawyers can garner positive press attention for the pro bono work they do. Some publications, such as *The American Lawyer*, actually rank firms by the volume of pro bono work done yearly.

Professional Development and Personal Satisfaction

Finally, firms recognize that pro bono work can help attorneys at all levels develop professionally while getting a great deal of meaning and personal satisfaction from their work.

Particularly for a more junior associate, pro bono offers many benefits:

Learning how to get things done in the firm. Depending on how your employer's pro bono program is structured (or not), you may have to bring in a new project to the firm, go through the process of getting the project approved by those in the firm who approve all new business, ensure that there are no legal or business conflicts that the project

---

3. *Millennials Want Skills-Based Involvement with Charities*, THE NONPROFIT TIMES (Dec. 19, 2016), http:// www.thenonprofittimes.com/news-articles/millennials -want-skills-based-involvement-charities/.

might pose, draft a retention letter between the client and the firm, and perhaps even develop a budget of the expected costs of taking on the project. These steps may be challenging to go through the first time, but by doing so, you will learn more about the business of the firm and how these important administrative tasks are handled. You will have greater insight into the steps that partners must take when they want to bring in new business, and you will also get to meet key administrative staff who can be tremendously helpful with all kinds of issues.

Valuable networking. Just by going through the steps of opening a new project at the firm, you are already meeting new people you might otherwise not have had the chance to meet until later in your tenure with the firm. Pro bono gives you the chance to **network** within your firm. Because pro bono matters tend to be leanly staffed, you may be working directly with your partner supervisor. This is a great opportunity to get to know a more senior person at the firm and to demonstrate your abilities to him or her. If you do a good job on the case, that partner may ask you to work on additional matters and may recommend you to fellow partners within the firm. Provided that the case or matter allows for this, you may even want to ask a partner outside of your primary practice area to supervise you, if he or she has a practice about which you'd be interested in learning. The pro bono matter you work on may even require lawyers with different areas of expertise, which will further allow you to work with people across a variety of practices.

Pro bono also gives you a chance to find people in the firm who share your interests and even your values. And partners who are known to regularly supervise associates on pro bono matters just tend to be nice. They may enjoy mentoring more junior associates and understand how to provide them with good guidance on projects while letting the associate take the lead.

Networking within your community is equally important. Pro bono work gives you an easy way to meet professionals outside of your firm. Your pro bono case may have been referred to the firm by a legal aid organization. By getting involved in that organization's work, attending their events, and even serving on a junior board, you'll be meeting more like-minded lawyers in your city and potentially open up opportunities to take on greater leadership roles in your community. Your employer should look favorably on this engagement outside the firm, as it is an early indicator that you may be partner material. And since you may leave your current firm for another employer within a few years, meeting lawyers from other organizations can better position you to be able to make such a move.

Skills, skills, skills. A pro bono case is a chance for you to take the lead on the matter. It's your chance to learn how to manage up, down, and sideways. You'll need to keep your partner supervisor informed of progress on the matter, all deadlines, and give her sufficient notice in order to be able to review all of your work product, attend client meetings, and any court calls. If other associates are helping on the case, you'll need to coordinate with them, and you'll also get important management experience working with legal secretaries and paralegals who may be involved.

And of course, you'll be learning new legal skills—intake and assessment, strategy and execution, fact gathering, drafting, preparing a witness, standing up in court, closing a transaction, listening skills, being accessible—all of which are critical ones to be used every day in your practice. The more you use them, the more confident you will become.

You'll feel good. If the professional development pro bono can offer doesn't convince you, remember that pro bono can just help you feel good about being a lawyer. Life as a new associate in a law firm can be very stressful, and the work you'll do may be very far removed from how you imagined using your legal skills in law school. Taking on a pro bono case gives you the chance to use your legal skills to make a huge impact on the life of an individual who otherwise couldn't afford a lawyer. By helping someone win asylum, for example, you might—quite literally—be saving someone's life.

How (and When) to Get Involved

Now that you are convinced that doing pro bono work is good for you, let's discuss how and when to get involved. As was mentioned at the start of this chapter, it's a good idea to get involved with pro bono work right away. You may be tempted to think, "I'll start when I have more time." You will never have more time than the time you have as a new associate. By taking on a pro bono project from the outset, you'll learn how to build pro bono into your practice from the start. And you'll feel more comfortable taking on a large project or a project in an area in which you aren't familiar if you have started early.

If your firm has an established pro bono program, the individual who runs that program can help you identify the right project and get you started. If your employer allows for pro bono work but doesn't have a defined program with suggested projects, your state's or city's bar association is a good starting point for possible pro bono projects. You might also do an Internet search for legal aid organizations in your city; most will provide instructions for attorneys looking to provide pro bono services.

Working with a legal aid organization that has an established pro bono program for volunteer lawyers is a good idea. These organizations will usually screen clients first to ensure that they actually have a legal claim or issue, and that they are an appropriate pro bono client for a volunteer who is new to pro bono. Look for organizations that offer on-demand or live training for the type of project you'd like to do, along with reference materials, sample documents, etc. In addition, ask the organization whether there is an expert attorney on staff who is available to ask questions, provide feedback and guidance to you, and review your work, if possible.

Considerations for Choosing a Project

How Much Time Do I Have to Devote to a New Matter?

If you aren't sure what your workload will be like starting out, volunteering regularly at a brief advice clinic is a great first step. Legal advice clinics are usually held on set days for a defined period of time. You'll still be practicing important lawyering skills and providing a valuable service, but you'll be able to volunteer on a schedule that has defined starting and stopping points. Legal aid organizations in your city will usually offer legal clinics in which any type of lawyer can participate, and they will usually offer some type of live or on-demand training. Often expert lawyers from the organization will be on hand during the clinic if you have questions, so it's a low-risk way to start. Because of the controlled environment and time period, they are a particularly good option if you work in a small firm or practice group.

If you are taking on a full-scope project from an organization, be sure to ask how many hours they estimate the project will require. You should expect to spend more time on the project if you are new to the work. You will also want to understand what deadlines may be involved and any other issues that may affect timing. Be sure to speak with your firm partners or direct supervisors to ensure they are comfortable with the time estimate for the work.

Will This Matter Require Travel or Other Expenses?

Consider the costs needed for the matter, such as filing fees, messenger costs, expert fees, etc. Some legal aid organizations require out-of-pocket expenses to be covered by the client, and some may maintain a fund to pay for such costs. You'll want to check with your employer to determine what, if any, expenses it will cover before you commit to accepting a project.

Do I Speak the Same Language As My Client?

When choosing a project, you also want to consider whether you speak the same language as your client. If not, you'll want to determine whether you can readily access affordable translation services.

Who Else Should I Work With?

As a new attorney, you will want to be sure to work with a more senior lawyer who can provide guidance and supervision. It's also a good idea to team up with another associate to ensure you are providing consistent coverage on your project in the event you get too busy. Consult with your supervisor as to whether additional attorneys with any specific expertise should also join the team.

Do I Have Malpractice Insurance?

Finally, you should be sure that you are covered by malpractice insurance. Typically, a firm's malpractice insurance will cover pro bono work, and most legal aid agencies' policies cover attorneys who volunteer with them, but be sure to check.

Points to Remember When Working with Pro Bono Clients

Even though your client is not paying for legal services, it is critical to remember that you have an ethical duty to treat your client with the same duty of care that you would give to your paying clients. That means providing regular reports to your client, being responsive to their correspondence, including your supervising partner in decision-making and client correspondence, consulting lawyers with the necessary expertise, if needed, and above all, asking for help if you get stuck.

You should also be clear with your pro bono client about the scope of your work. Pro bono clients often have multiple legal issues, and it is important at the outset of your matter to set their expectations by explaining clearly to them what work you will, and won't, be doing for them. The scope of your work should also be clearly and narrowly defined in writing in the retention letter. When you have completed the work for the client, you should also send the client a letter indicating that the matter has been completed and that you are no longer the client's attorney.

Your client may never have worked with a lawyer before and may not work with you in the same way that a typical paying client works. For example, your client may not have easy access to a computer or the Internet. They may be difficult to reach—their phones may be disconnected, they may move frequently, or have inconsistent work schedules. It may be hard for them to meet you at your office or during regular work hours.

When you first meet with your client, discuss the client's responsibility to keep you informed about his or her contact information. You may want to get alternate phone numbers and emergency contacts, whether it be through the client's work, friends, or family. Ask the client how they prefer to communicate, the best times they can be reached, and their work schedules, so you can schedule any key appearances during their days off. If your pro bono client will need to send you documents, give your client stamped, self-addressed envelopes in different sizes to make it easier for them to send you the documents you need.

Finally, being a good advocate for your client requires you to be "culturally competent." Be sensitive to the fact that your life experiences may be very different from your client's, due to any number of factors, including race, gender, ethnicity, economic status, immigration status, language, birth order, physical characteristics, LGBTQ status, age, etc. Understanding the cultural differences that can arise during communication with your client can make you a much more effective lawyer. Be sure to ask the legal aid organization you work with for available resources and guidance for working with a particular client population. You can also find a number of trainings and articles online on cultural competency in pro bono representation.

Integrating pro bono work into your practice from the beginning is a wonderful way to provide meaningful help to others while growing personally and professionally. The benefits you will gain from your service will far outweigh the hours you commit. And ensuring that those who cannot afford to pay for legal services still have access to quality legal representation protects the civil justice system for everyone.

Chapter 8

Embracing Technology and Innovation in Legal Practice

Chris Boyd, Amy Halverson, and
Serena Miller*

Introduction

Let's go back twenty years and imagine that you're a first
year associate in 1998 . . .

- You go to your office every day. "Telecommuting"
  does not exist.

- Even though Apple just released candy-colored
  iMacs, your computer is a large, heavy black or gray
  Windows desktop. No firm-issued laptop for you.

---

*   At Wilson Sonsini Goodrich & Rosati, Chris Boyd is the Chief
     Knowledge and Talent Officer, Amy Halverson is Director of
     Knowledge Management, Research & Information Services, and
     Serena Miller is the Director of Professional Development.

- Your mobile phone is a Nokia brick or Motorola flip. You use it for phone calls—that's it.

- Your firm has fax machines in every wing. You use them frequently.

- Google just launched its Internet search engine and is competing fiercely for market share with Alta Vista, Excite, and Yahoo! But sadly, within your firm, "enterprise search" consists of walking the halls looking for relevant deal-closing volumes.

Now aren't you glad you're starting your legal career in 2018 rather than 1998? Because technology generally and legal practice tools specifically have changed so much for the better over the past twenty years, you will be far more productive and will likely enjoy practicing law much more than your predecessors. You will be able to do all of the following far more efficiently than they could: find sample documents; locate legal precedent; run deal closings; do discovery; do due diligence; and do many other typical first year associate tasks. There are many ways you can harness legal technology and innovation to rapidly develop your capabilities and become a competent and contented practitioner. And this chapter will show you how.

Before diving into specifics, two pieces of advice for your first year as an associate:

1. Learn as much as you can about the actual practice of law. Despite wanting to believe otherwise, graduation from law school does not make you a qualified attorney. That only comes with years of observation, practice, and adopting good habits.

2. Learn how to provide value as quickly as possible. The more proficient you become at tasks, the easier they are to perform, the more accurately you com-

plete them, and you then start building a reputation as a trusted and valued resource for those with whom you work.

Market and Technology Trends Supporting Increased Innovation and Better Technology Usage

Now, let's explore some ways you can harness legal technology and innovation to provide that value. Fortunately, the wind is at your back, as several trends are driving law firms to innovate more and use technology better.

Client demand for value. Clients are asking their law firms and other legal service providers to deliver more value, including increasing the efficiency, predictability, and transparency of their services and fees. In response, law firms are moving away from the billable hour revenue model and pricing services using fixed fees and other alternative arrangements. To do this profitably, firms are harnessing project management techniques and innovative technology to price services more competitively (including via fixed fees) and deliver them more predictably and efficiently. For you, as a first year associate, mastering these techniques and tools can improve the quality of your work experience and increase the number and variety of your matters.

Recent technology innovations that speed up core first-year tasks. Tools that use natural language processing, machine learning, image recognition, and document automation have reduced the attorney time required to perform mundane junior associate tasks such as document review in litigation, and due diligence, deal document, and signing management in corporate transactions. This complementary category of legal technology is expanding rapidly to encompass facilitated legal work such as research and deal term analysis and comparison. As a first year attorney, these tools enable you quickly to advance to the "lawyerly" work and generally do not require a significant investment in time learning the underlying technology—these tools will become as ubiquitous as Word and Excel.

Recent technology innovations that require data literacy. Another set of complementary tools can surface many types of data about legal events, characteristics, outcomes, and trends. As a first year attorney, you should cultivate the skill of connecting the dots between the data universe and the specifics of your case; that ability will help you tremendously. For example, if a new patent case is filed against your client, use these tools to find out how the assigned judge typically rules in patent disputes and at what stage in the litigation, how successful the plaintiff and the plaintiff's counsel have been in prior matters and what motion strategy they have used, if and how the patent has been litigated before, and the identities of the expert witnesses supporting the winning side.

Opportunity to build self-service legal expertise tools. Great strides are being made with "self-service" online tools that use expert systems and artificial intelligence to solve legal problems ranging from fighting parking ticket infractions to performing complex regulatory compliance assessments—and, perhaps most needed, providing individuals who otherwise cannot afford attorneys with access to justice. Innovators are starting to use blockchain technology to enable self-authenticating "smart contract" platforms that create binding legal contracts. Once you've mastered the tools described above, you may have the opportunity to work with application development teams to design these types of tools, which combine legal expertise with user experience expertise, platform scalability and security, and an awareness of the implicit biases that can inadvertently be hard-coded into predictive systems, among other things.

Ways to Capitalize on Technology and Process Innovations

Before diving deep into artificial intelligence, start by mastering project management, process optimization, and time management. Record your time daily and routinely update your supervising attorneys on progress and status. There are a variety of tools available to help you do this quickly and accurately, so get in the habit of using them. Beyond just utilizing Outlook and other tools your firm may use for task management, there are tools that help you track your time and even create a script of commonly used time entry phrases. Familiarizing yourself with project management process improvement principles will also pay dividends both for client work and your own personal career development (note that PLI's online curriculum includes a seminar entitled Project Management for Lawyers).

As for routine drafting and editing of documents, find out what add-ons your firm may have to Word and other Microsoft Office products. It is likely that more than spellcheck is available to you—your firm may license products that can flag inconsistencies in defined words in agreements, or link to a clause bank repository. Ask questions and get to know the people who train attorneys on technology. Volunteer to be an "early adopter" for new tools. Also, make sure you know all the ins and outs of redlining, OCRing (optical character recognition), converting documents between formats, Excel formulas and pivot tables—these seemingly small things can render huge efficiencies, and you don't want to have to rely on an assistant or paralegal to do them for you.

As for the more interesting ways to leverage emerging legal technology, start with data literacy. You can find all kinds of data literacy and analytics guides and courses online. Learn the difference between structured and unstructured data, the whys and hows of data scrubbing, and the various sources of data available to you. The most effective use of data for process improvement and strategic decision-making is often a combination of external data and internal data, from your firm's own business systems, so learn what those systems are and what is in them.

Another area to explore is design thinking, an emerging discipline for lawyers and those who develop technology tools with lawyers. In the legal context, design thinking prioritizes the needs and experience of the end user (your client) in designing ways to deliver legal services, involves early prototyping and multiple iterations, and results in a service model that is simple, intuitive, and even pleasurable for the client. Some law schools are introducing design thinking courses and labs into their curriculum, and legal design thinking resources can be found online.

Your experience as a first year attorney will undoubtedly be different from that of your firm's partners and even senior associates. You will be able to use tools and systems to complete low-level work and more quickly get to the substantive part of being a lawyer. But keep in mind, no technology, no matter how advanced, can substitute for good legal judgment and sound decision-making. You may only be in your first year of practice but you are an accredited lawyer practicing law. And the buck ultimately stops with you.

Ways to Capitalize on Professional Development Innovations

There are other ways that you as a first year can capitalize on law firm innovation beyond the application of technology. One important area is professional development. Just as technology used to involve bulky desktops and fax machines, old-school law firm learning could only be described as a drag: live lectures in a stuffy conference room, taught by an aging firm patriarch who read the same presentation year after year. Law firm internal training then followed the model of traditional classroom learning, as no other model existed at the time. And then, a revolution! We got PowerPoint. Then, in 2005, three guys from PayPal decided on-demand video was the wave of the future (that would be YouTube). And somewhere along the way, we realized that in-house expert practitioners were more effective teachers of substantive topics than were the oldest citizens of the firm.

But it didn't stop there. Once theories of adult learning gained traction and the concept that people retain information differently took root, a door opened to using technology to teach in new and innovative ways. While we still have the option of traditional classroom learning, we also use much newer, innovative, and more effective formats, such as: gamified exercises to teach skill topics (see: Training the Street); quick-hit training to offer guidance on specific drill down topic areas (see: most on-demand learning portals); "flipping the classroom" allowing for class time to be spent working through simulated exercises rather than focus on theoretical learning first and the need for potentially elusive real-life experience to reinforce the lesson (see: Hotshot); and a veritable plethora of on-demand learning sites that make it easy to seek and immediately gain knowledge on some level in every legal area (see: PLI, Biotech Primer). If your firm employs such formats, take full advantage of their learning potential.

Firms have also applied this ability to provide legal learning in different ways to the important area of professional skills. Attorneys need more than substantive legal prowess to be successful; they need knowledge in areas such as business acumen, communications, leadership, management, and resilience. Because our clients value these skills highly, our firm has created entire learning curricula dedicated to increasing associates' capabilities in these areas, and has hired outside experts to train attorneys in them, both in groups and via one-on-one coaching. Take advantage of your firm's professional skills training offerings, as this type of skills development can elevate you from good to great.

That said, while you should absolutely capitalize on innovations in professional development, the traditional apprentice model still works well for many junior associates. Look for opportunities to learn from the most experienced practitioners at your firm. Ask people what they use to help maximize efficiencies. Use this as a conversation to meet someone. Pick your audience wisely, of course, but if you can get time with one of your firm's legends to legitimately and genuinely ask what tools they use to help their practice, you will absolutely remember that conversation forever.

The Burden of Being Perceived As Tech-Savvy

A brief detour into the real world here: you come into law firms with a few labels on your back and chief among those is "Tech-Savvy." Mostly, this is fair because you have grown accustomed to using technology as a natural component of your learning experience. Please remember that there are people who are not as adept as you are at understanding the whys and wherefores, or seeing the benefits of certain applications. Be patient. Explain. Help them to understand. Be Obi-Wan.

Finally, a note on helping to modernize those around you. As concepts of efficiency improvement or creating more dynamic client interactions gain solid ground within law firms, there are a lot of new technologies being developed to help facilitate them. If you can get in front of anything, do so. If you have earned trusted advisor status by providing good quality and accurate work, you can leverage that reputation to make suggestions which might actually be paid attention to. Don't lose the opportunity to provide an additional value contribution. And think about how much more awesome you can help make a CLE or client-facing presentation.

If you have a friend developing an app (and who doesn't?) that would make any aspect of law firm life easier (except for the actual part of being a lawyer), find out more. Help your professional development team help everyone else. We love innovation suggestions!

Other Things First Year Associates Can Do to Benefit from—and Contribute to— Innovation

Once you've learned your firm's most innovative technology and capitalized on its innovative professional development, what else can you do as a first year associate to leverage your firm's legal technology and promote innovation? A few suggestions:

- Master the tools used most by junior associates as part of their daily workflow, particularly those for time entry, time and task management, and generation of work product. Invest the time needed to become facile in document formatting, redlining, Excel table structures and functions, and so on. Pay attention during your firm's first year associate orientation, which will teach you to use at least a few of them. Ask your firm's technology training team for their top tips beyond what they teach during the orientation. Ask also for any practice-specific tips; if you're a litigator, the tools you'll want to use may be different from those most useful to your corporate, patent, or antitrust colleagues.

- Learn how and where to find things within the firm, because supervising attorneys frequently ask first years to do this. Learn how to find useful internal templates and precedents, relevant past matters, and the firm's experts on topics your clients will care about. Most firms have harnessed innovative search technologies to some degree to help junior associates with these typical tasks.

- Learn also how to find things outside the firm. Most firms subscribe to useful external databases of case law, corporate and intellectual property filings, regulatory materials, how-to explanations, and other useful items. Find out from your firm's training classes and supervising attorneys the most common types of external things you'll be asked to find, then learn how to find them quickly. Your firm's research librarians and knowledge management specialists will be helpful allies here.

- Elevate your practice by fortifying your legal training with coursework in multi-disciplinary subjects relevant to technology and business practices. Learn basic principles of project management. Familiarize yourself with data and how to use it. Understand the similarities and differences between machine learning and natural language processing, as each are increasingly used in emerging legal technology and artificial intelligence tools. Look for opportunities for training on soft skills such as public speaking, business acumen, and leadership. Fortunately, advances in technology and learning theory have made a variety of learning platforms available to you to take coursework in these subjects.

And don't forget to keep up with innovations in technology that are important to your clients. Technology is changing the way all businesses run and even the nature of the businesses themselves. Being familiar with your client's business model, goals, and competitors will always improve your ability to be a trusted advisor to that client—and that includes the technology they use, build, or care about.

Once you've become an effective and efficient junior associate, you can also help your firm continue to innovate. Many firms have appointed a Chief Innovation Officer (CINO); if your firm has a CINO, get to know her or him and find out more about her/his work. CINO roles vary from firm to firm, but all bear responsibility for working with firm and practice group leadership to identify and implement process, role, and technology innovations that enable firms to deliver more value to clients. A CINO will usually have multiple projects under way and may value associate input and participation. The CINO may be called something else, so look for anyone who has an "innovation" title.

Even if your firm hasn't designated a formal innovation leader or chartered a formal innovation initiative, there will be innovation happening. If you'd like to help make law work better at your firm, or have suggestions for doing so, talk to the firm's Chief Information Officer (CIO) or the leaders of your firm's knowledge management and legal project management initiatives, as those people typically know which attorneys are most interested in innovation and process improvement, and can point you in the right direction. Some firms give billable hour credit for participation in these initiatives; take advantage of this.

Final Advice

All of that said, remember the two important pieces of advice we gave in the Introduction: before doing anything else, first learn as much as you can about the actual practice of law, and learn how to provide value as quickly as possible. If you do this, and thereby build your reputation and create internal demand for your time, you'll be in a much better position to contribute to the firm's innovation initiative. Good luck!

Chapter 9

Success for Diverse Lawyers

Chintan Amin[*]

Understand What Makes You Tick

Generally Applicable Advice Applies to You, Too

You've landed your first job at a large law firm, which many see as the pinnacle of achievement for those graduating from law school. But the first day you set foot in the office, you realize, "I don't look like any of these folks. My parents didn't belong to the same clubs their's did. I didn't attend the same private high schools they did." Many straight, white men certainly feel this way when they join BigLaw, but attorneys from outside the majority group are almost guaranteed to feel left out of this "club." And it can feel like membership in this "club" is the only path to a successful career in the law, meeting the right people, securing the right clients, and making partner.

---

[*]   Senior Counsel, Bayer U.S. LLC.

What can you, as a new attorney from a diverse background, do to get *yourself* into the club or to start re-shaping the club? How can you pass the trial by fire that is being a first year associate? There are a number of positive steps that a young lawyer can take to improve their chances of success at the law firm, whether your aim is to make partner or not. And many of these tips take advantage of your diversity and distinctiveness.

But before we get to those, you need to understand yourself and what makes you tick. Are you more comfortable in business casual or do you feel more professional in a suit? Do you thrive under pressure or do you need a little more space to work effectively? Do you need regular feedback during the course of a project or would you rather have only the final draft reviewed? Is your working style collaborative or individualistic? Knowing yourself will help you to tailor not only the advice in this chapter but the rest of this book as well to maximize your potential.

Taking stock of your own professional style will help you determine how you can fit into your practice group's or your firm's culture. Within a single law firm, practice group cultures can range widely and even differ significantly among partners within the same practice group. The sooner you figure out whether your style can mesh with that of the senior attorneys assigning work (or of the practice group or firm), the better chance you have of figuring out what you need to do to succeed at that firm. You may eventually realize that your first firm is not for you. This realization stands on its own as a win, because it puts you on course to find a situation that better suits your style.

You may be thinking to yourself, "everything in this chapter so far applies to majority attorneys as well as diverse attorneys," and you would be right. But these are the foundational precepts that span race, ethnicity, gender identity, and sexual orientation. No matter whether you heed the advice later on in this chapter, if you don't get the "blocking and tackling" above and in the rest of this book right, you won't succeed at BigLaw or, frankly, in the profession as a whole.

Do You Feel Like an Imposter?

I immigrated to the United States from India as a child and wound up working as a first year associate in a large law firm in the southeastern United States. For many years, even after progressing through the associate ranks and making partner there, I felt as though I was on the outside looking in. This wasn't the result of any shortcomings on the firm's part; it was a welcoming firm that set the standard among its peers for encouraging diversity. But the feeling was real, and more honestly put, I sometimes felt like I was pulling one over on my peers and colleagues. It turns out, I'm not alone.

A recent article in the *New York Times* explores "Imposter Syndrome" and how it disproportionately affects minority professionals.[1] This term was devised in 1978 by two psychologists, Pauline Clance and Suzanne Imes, to describe an "internal experience of intellectual phoniness" that they noted among professional women. In their research, these women, no matter their academic credentials or professional acclaim, felt like outsiders among their peers. More recent research has shown that while "Imposter Syndrome" exists across all demographics, researchers believe it is more prevalent among minority groups.

---

1. Kristin Wong, *Dealing with Impostor Syndrome When You're Treated as an Impostor*, N.Y. TIMES (June 6, 2018), https://www. nytimes.com/2018/06/12/smarter-living/dealing-with-impostor-syndrome-when-youre-treated-as-an-impostor.html (accessed June 14, 2018).

At the risk of sounding a depressing note, a researcher at the University of Texas, Austin found that imposterism was "an even greater predictor of negative mental health outcomes in minorities than discrimination."[2] The researcher, Professor Kevin Cokley, explains that while discrimination doesn't necessarily cause imposterism, he found that imposterism can exacerbate the feeling of isolation felt by diverse professionals who have felt the impact of discrimination. The sense of isolation spurred by imposterism can be a heavy yoke and can not only hurt the "imposter" but also stymie growth and innovation in the organization.

Success Factors for Diverse Attorneys

Overcoming Imposterism at Your Firm

"Being alone puts you in a circumstance where you're not only questioning yourself, but also looking for agreement in others," according to LinkedIn's Head of Global Diversity, Inclusion and Belonging, Rosanna Durruthy.[3] This feeling can undermine your self-confidence, dull your assertiveness, and hurt your professional experience. Imagine yourself at a strategy meeting to plan out the next phase of a big transaction. As a less-experienced associate, you've been getting your hands dirty, reviewing key schedules, and researching new developments in the law. You recognize that the client may realize certain advantages if it tweaks certain aspects of the deal structure. If you are not confident, if you feel like an imposter, and bring that hesitance into the meeting with you, it can cost you, your firm, and the client.

As you can see, it's not only important for your professional growth and personal well-being to slay this dragon,

---

2. *Id.*
3. *Id.*

but it will improve the value your employer will realize from your work. Luckily, the remedies recommended by experts to reduce the effects of imposterism are a good fit for lawyers from diverse backgrounds and young lawyers generally. It's always helpful to have a support group of professionals who understand your background and can empathize with your experience. While we are all unique, it's easier to open up with people whose experiences you share. These days, many employers have affinity groups, also known as employee resource groups, for various groups of employees. For example, these groups may bring together African-American employees, employees with disabilities, veterans, or women. These groups can be used by employees to compare notes on employer policies and employee experiences. They can act as a support group and mentorship program. They help you navigate your workplace, by learning from and collaborating with others.

Viewing diversity as a key business goal, the company where I serve as in-house counsel established an Asian-American employee resource group to help promote awareness of Asian-Americans among the employee base and management. Recent research has found that, while Asian-Americans are in some ways an extremely successful minority group economically, a glass ceiling has resulted in them being significantly underrepresented among corporate leadership.[4] Indeed, a recent study in the *Harvard Business Review* found that Asian-Americans are the *least* likely to make it to management positions.[5] As chair of the

---

4. *See, e.g.*, Buck Gee & Denise Peck, *Asian Americans Are the Least Likely Group in the U.S. to Be Promoted to Management*, HARV. BUS. REV. (2018), https://hbr.org/2018/05/asian-americans-are-the-least-likely-group-in-the-u-s-to-be-promoted-to-management (accessed June 18, 2018).

5. *Id.*

local chapter of this group, I organized a panel discussion among several Asian-American leaders in our company to explore their career paths and the tools they used to reach their positions.

The setting fostered an open and honest examination of corporate culture and our own home cultures. For example, does the deference to age and hierarchy in some Asian cultures result in a reluctance among Asian-Americans to assert themselves? What can the company do to make its Asian-American employees feel more comfortable about exhibiting leadership qualities? And how can we, as Asian-Americans, develop in this area? This discussion would have been much more difficult in a different setting with a different audience. In the end, however, attendees and participants found the discussion enlightening and useful.

If your employer does not have an employee resource group, you could consider forming your own. For example, even an informal lunch group of Latinx attorneys could generate great conversation, important ideas, and useful tips. In fact, most employee resource groups start out as informal meetings of like-minded employees. Your law school or college may also have affinity alumni networks in your city. Social media platforms like LinkedIn could also offer an opportunity to interact with like-minded folks, albeit less directly. The point is that finding a support group of people with similar life experiences can help diverse lawyers have a sense of belonging. Additionally, in a pragmatic sense, it increases your connections and the "people you know," which is essential to progressing in a firm.

Join an Affinity Bar Association to Meet Like-Minded Attorneys

Affinity bar associations also provide a valuable resource for diverse lawyers seeking professional advice and personal friendships. Affinity bars exist to connect attorneys to others that share similar life experiences or cultural backgrounds. They provide support for attorneys looking to share experiences and an opportunity for professional networking. They can also provide speaking opportunities earlier in your career than some of the mainstream bar associations. Recognition within these bar associations can provide a positive notoriety in the firm and a springboard to additional opportunities.

These days, there are a wide variety of affinity bar associations, some large and some small. In fact, in some localities, there may be an even larger number of affinity bars that focus on demographics more likely to live in that area. Many of these groups have annual meetings of the national organization while offering local chapters for more convenient, nearby meetings. Local groups are a great place to start; they usually plan more frequent meetings than their national counterparts. And following up on a great conversation with a one-on-one coffee is a lot easier. And of course, it's easier to attend something down the street than in another state.

Developing a rapport with local attorneys with similar life experiences to yours is a wonderful professional tool. You can use this opportunity to build an informal networking group and just make new social friends. But once you've done that, consider attending a meeting of the bar association's national affiliate. There, you'll find a much larger and more diverse group of potential contacts. You may meet a future client or a referral source. Additionally, the national meetings are often set up as continuing education conferences, which will give you an opportunity to speak as well.

While not an exhaustive list, some of the affinity bar associations are:

- Dominican Bar Association
- Haitian Lawyers Association

- Hispanic National Bar Association
- Minority Corporate Counsel Association
- National Asian Pacific American Bar Association
- National Association of Muslim Lawyers
- National Association of Women Lawyers
- National Bar Association
- National Filipino American Lawyers Association
- National LGBT Bar Association
- National Native American Bar Association
- South Asian Bar Association of North America

Some attorneys will find natural fits within multiple affinity bars: a Pakistani-American attorney would find familiarity within the South Asian Bar Association of North America (SABA), the National Association of Muslim Lawyers, and the National Asian Pacific American Bar Association. Each of these organizations provides a different cross-section of American (and in the case of SABA, North American) attorneys that may share experiences with our Pakistani-American friend. Why not try all three to find the best fit?

Don't Ignore Mainstream Bar Associations for Networking Opportunities

While affinity bars are an important way to connect with similar attorneys, don't ignore the more mainstream professional organizations. The American Bar Association (ABA) and many state bar associations have Young Lawyer Divisions (YLDs) where younger attorneys from all backgrounds can hone leadership skills, make valuable future contacts among contemporaries, and organize events. These organizations are typically open to lawyers under forty or who have only been practicing a few years. This limited membership allows you to be a bigger fish in a smaller pond, taking charge of programs and developing the types of professional interpersonal skills that will come in handy in your career. You will also be able to make solid bonds with peers who may provide referrals, future business when they go in-house, or valuable contacts when you're looking to make that lateral move.

While YLDs provide opportunities for lawyers to get their feet wet in leadership positions and make contacts within the same age range, you also want to develop a reputation among lawyers in your practice area. State bar and ABA sections provide opportunities for you to network with attorneys within your own practice area, to raise your profile among your peers, and to develop deeper expertise. As a new attorney progresses in their career, active membership in these sections will often lead to speaking opportunities at bar events and elsewhere. These speaking opportunities will provide you with the ability to rub shoulders with knowledgeable attorneys within your field and to get yourself in front of potential clients.

Seek Out Mentors to Help You Understand Firm Culture

Finding a mentor is yet another way to improve your chances for success, whether you're a member of a minority group or of the majority. Senior attorneys will want to help you acclimate to your new surroundings, and many firms offer formal mentorship programs for new attorneys. Remember that when you walk into your firm on your first day, it has already spent a significant amount of money recruiting you and will spend a lot of money training and paying you. The last thing the partners want is for you to fail. They have a vested financial interest in your staying at the firm for at least a few years. Moreover, any rational partner (and, of course, there are irrational partners out there) understands that a happy associate is a productive associate is a profitable associate. So, the firm not only wants you to stay, but also to stay happy with your circumstances on the job.

Finding a mentor with shared cultural and life experiences is a great way to break the ice and find somebody who's already dealt with what you are going through. For example, a young woman might find the mentorship of a more senior female valuable, especially when discussing work-life balance with a young family. An African-American mentor could help a young black attorney understand how he can get the best work opportunities from the mostly majority senior associates and partners in his group. Of course, a mentor from within your own firm is great, but you may have to look elsewhere, which is another reason why joining an affinity bar association may come in handy. Many offer formal and informal mentorship opportunities.

Your Mentor May Not Look Like You . . . and That's OK

While it makes sense that a mentor would have similar experiences to your own, one of the most powerful benefits of mentorship is the ability to emulate the behaviors that made the mentor successful. But you may find that the only other Indian-American attorney in your firm is in a very different practice area or has a different work style than you. Don't foreclose the opportunity to learn from somebody just because they do not look like you or share similar life experiences. Inherent in the definition of the word "minority" is the mathematical fact that you may not find as many people like you at your firm. Don't forego the opportunity to develop meaningful relationships with non-minority attorneys who want to see you succeed. Doing so could throw away a real opportunity to further yourself and your career; more often than not, senior attorneys want to help all of their associates succeed.

When I joined my firm, one of my mentors there was a partner thirty years my senior. This blonde-haired, fair-skinned partner shared few common life experiences with me, except that we both graduated from the same law school. However, we shared a similar work style and I admired his informal professionalism. Thus, I spent time with him, and learned how he was able to maximize his strengths and overcome or cover for his weaknesses. He drilled down on me when he thought I wasn't attentive enough to details, a weakness he saw in himself. And he celebrated my accomplishments. As I progressed through the ranks, he and I would recruit at our alma mater and foremost among his priorities was to find a diverse group of candidates to call back for interviews. His passion for doing good was inspiring and, despite our superficial differences, following in his footsteps gave me a broader professional perspective.

While formal mentorship opportunities are certainly useful, you should also look to make more informal, almost social contacts with attorneys at your firm. If your firm has an attorney dining room or cafeteria, look to sit with attorneys you don't know. This is an opportunity to find out what others do and learn about interdisciplinary work that you may find interesting. Perhaps the partner you're sitting with from the corporate group has an interesting client or project that you'd like to work on. Developing more social bonds across practice areas means that you might move up the list of younger associates they contact for a new matter.

This is also a way to develop an internal client base: attorneys in the firm who view you as a reliable expert on certain areas of law. Providing good client service and excellent work product is the most important thing a young attorney can do, but it's also necessary to let folks know what you know. A mid-level associate who can stay busy billing hours without being bottle-fed by the partners in her group is usually a well-regarded associate. This is true not only because it reduces their headache but also because it is a sign the associate will be able to develop external business on her own, which is obviously a key point of evaluation during partnership decisions.

Selling Yourself Is Not a Bad Thing

You will have recognized that a number of the suggestions above involve opportunities to get experience and notoriety outside of the typical flow of work within the firm. It is extremely important for your future that you ensure that firm management is aware of your accomplishments. There are at least two reasons for this: first, you deserve credit for your hard work and achievement, and second, people are busy and your success may not be visible to them.

In fact, experts on imposterism strongly suggest keeping a record of positive feedback and accomplishments. Dr. Cokley recommends keeping a diary to document the positives. "[G]o back and look at all those instances in which you've gotten good feedback, where you've been told you've done a good job and done something well,"[6] he said. This can provide a somewhat more balanced view of yourself.

Not only will documenting your accomplishments help exorcise the imposterism demons, you can also use it to develop an "experience catalog." An experience catalog is useful in three ways. First, you can use it to determine what types of work you have gotten and what experience level you have. For example, are you a second-year litigation associate who has not yet been involved in witness prepa-

---

6.   *See* Wong, *supra* note 1.

ration? Or a fourth year who has not handled a witness on her own? Keeping track of your experiences will help you fill in the holes and ensure you get a broad enough range of work to keep you on track at the firm. Second, you can use your experience catalog to develop your resume if you want to make a lateral move or to go in-house. Third, you owe it to yourself to ensure your accomplishments are known to senior lawyers at your firm. Obviously, you should be tactful in your methods; sharing good news at the wrong time or in the wrong way could make you look like a blowhard. But sharing good news the right way at the right time is essential to your progression.

The experience catalog is a useful reminder of positive experiences that you can share. Don't be afraid to bring up the deposition where you got the opposing expert to admit his methods were suspect when you're talking to a senior partner. This will stick in her mind and maybe result in additional work or a development opportunity.

While all young associates face challenges, a minority attorney at a big firm has unique difficulties. Overcoming them will depend on taking an honest account of your own needs. However, many employers and the profession as a whole are keenly aware that they need to do more to help diverse attorneys succeed. Take advantage of mentoring opportunities to learn the best work habits and honestly analyze your career. Get active in both affinity bar associations and employee resource groups to leverage the experiences of others to your advantage. Don't forget about mainstream bar associations to build your network more generally. And finally, make sure you track and publicize your accomplishments to ensure that your successes are properly appreciated. That's one way you will feel like you belong in this club while you make your own club that you can use to help the next diverse associate that comes along.

Chapter 10

Preparing for a Status Meeting: Presenting Your Work in Person

Catharine Du Bois*

Junior associates are regularly asked to update a supervising attorney or a team on the status of a project and to do so in a face-to-face meeting. Your supervisor might ask you for an update for any number of reasons: she might be preparing for a strategy meeting or a client call, he may want to follow up to make sure you are on the right track, or she might want to hear the results of your analysis to make a decision about next steps. No matter the reason, your supervisors are looking for the same thing: to be updated on your project and to clarify next steps.

How you present yourself and your work in these face-to-face meetings is as important to your professional persona as your final product. But many associates mistake the

---

* Professor of Legal Research and Writing; Program Director, Writing Persuasive Briefs, National Institute for Trial Advocacy.

casual atmosphere of a status meeting as permission to be underprepared and disorganized. In fact, these status—or "where are we on this?"—meetings are crucial professional opportunities to impress.

The ability to present your work clearly and cogently isn't innate; it isn't the born genius of a lucky few. It's a learnable skill. And the difference between the associate that masters this skill and one that doesn't is the difference between an associate who seems organized and put-together and an associate who seems flustered and unprepared. Thus, mastering this skill early in your career is essential to being perceived as a competent attorney.

This chapter will provide you a process for preparing for a status meeting so that you can be ready to present yourself well.

Before You Prepare

Whether you have a few hours or a week before the status meeting, effective preparation is essential. To present yourself cogently and clearly, you must spend time organizing your results and advice in a way that at once provides a conclusion and explains how you reached that conclusion.

But before you can start to prepare, you have to know what you are preparing for. Before you begin, determine the answers to three basic questions: what is the purpose of the meeting, what kind of meeting is it, and who will be there? These questions will help you understand the meeting's scope and content so that you can prepare effectively.

The Purpose

Generally, the purpose of a status meeting is for you—the expert on the project—to summarize your work. As such, the purpose depends in part on what your original assignment was. However, a secondary purpose, one that will hone and refine the way you prepare, is the meeting request itself.

First, return to the original assignment or your notes from the original meeting to confirm that you have a firm grasp on what you were asked to do and that your work to this point has been on point. Often the exact assignment gets lost in the details of your research or preparation or fact review. What started as a "could we include a limitation of liability provision" easily becomes a draft of the provision. Although the draft provision might be the next step (and it's great to be a step ahead!), you'll still be expected to explain to your supervisor why it is the best next step.

Second, clarify the meeting request. Are you being asked to give a general status report or are you being asked a specific question that relates to your overall project? If you aren't sure, clarify. Better to ask that follow-up question than to present something that isn't relevant or useful.

The Audience

If you can, find out who will be present—just the assigning partner or the whole project team? By knowing who will be there, you can figure out how much information the audience has already and how familiar they are with the case, the facts, the specific project, and the authority.

The Format

Learn as much as you can about the meeting itself. For example, find out how much time you will have and where will the meeting will be. If this is a meeting between just you and the partner in your partner's office, you should prepare to lead a detailed meeting, but you might not need to provide as much context. However, if it is a team meeting where many people are providing status updates, you should prepare to effectively but briefly summarize your part in broader terms that a less-informed audience can understand.

Purpose, audience, and format will help you determine exactly what you need to present, how much detail you should go into, and what the expectations are for the content.

Prepare for the Meeting

Once you understand what you are preparing for, you can begin to prepare the substance. First, review your research and your work to make sure you understand the assignment from all angles. Next, anticipate the questions your audience might have. Focusing on what the listener needs to know to understand your conclusion helps identify the necessary framework and context.

With the purpose and the framework in mind, create an outline that will guide you during your meeting. The outline should organize your material into clear and logical talking points and it should be in a format that you can refer to easily, without getting lost or creating a distraction.

Your outline should include the following:

Introduction

Briefly remind your audience of what you are working on and how the assignment came up. Then clearly state the purpose and scope of your discussion.

Your purpose will often best be stated as a conclusion about what your research or assessment means for next steps in the project. It could be what language you suggest for a contract provision, what advice you suggest for the executive summary, or what conclusion you've reached about a legal research question.

The scope is about where you are in the project and what this meeting will cover. For example, it could be that you've reached a conclusion about some aspects of the assignment but need further information or more time to complete other aspects of the assignment.

Orienting Information and Roadmap

Orient the audience with any necessary background. Even if the audience is familiar with the case (which isn't always the case), it is still helpful to review background so that everyone is clear and has the same understanding of what's relevant.

Next, provide the roadmap, which explains how the meeting will be organized. The roadmap should reinforce the scope and provide a clear framework. For example, "the three-part test requires that the court find (1) . . . (2) . . . and (3) . . . ." or "we should advise a shift in management for four reasons: . . ." or "four principal decisions need to be reached to move forward: . . . ."

You could even provide an agenda. A written agenda looks professional and provides a visual outline for your audience, which is a great comfort to the listener. An agenda can also help remind the audience what the limits of your assignment were and can head off any frustration caused by an incorrect assumption of what you should know.

The Substance

Once you have outlined the purpose and scope, and provided the roadmap, prepare the substance. The substance should include the following:

1. *The authority.* Explain the applicable law or authority succinctly and first. Generally, your audience needs your conclusion to be based on authority. For a legal analysis conclusion, the authority is case law or statute; for advice to the client, the authority could include corporate policies; for an agreement, it could include client goals.

   For a face-to-face meeting, you do not need to provide a detailed discussion of the authority, but you do need to ground your discussion in a rule or principle. Though you should be prepared to answer questions about the authority, you should not plan to explain in detail unless you get questions. To a listener who is eagerly anticipating your analysis, an overly detailed description of the authority can seem irrelevant and off scope.

2. *The material facts.* The facts are the anchor for your discussion; it's what makes your circumstance unique. Even where you believe the audience knows the case well, highlight the relevant facts to make sure it's clear which facts are relevant to your discussion. Without that, it will be difficult for the audience to see the relevance of the analysis you are presenting. Also, it is essential that you know the facts and understand the significance of each fact better than anyone else in the room.

3. *How the authority applies to the facts (and supports your conclusion).* This is the crux: this is where you convince your supervisor that you have done the assignment fully and competently. Use the authority you described to show how the authority applies to the specific circumstances and how it supports your conclusion or advice. Also, explain any weaknesses

or gaps in facts or research. If you are waiting for more discovery or it is an early stage in your project, explain what still needs to be done and what outcomes are possible.

Conclusion and Next Steps

Conclude with a general recap of your conclusion or advice and recommend the next steps. You are the expert on this subject; your advice is based on study and consideration. As such, your audience expects and wants your recommendation.

The Meeting

While your preparation and outline are essential, it is substance only. And a successful meeting depends not only on the substance but also on how you conduct the meeting. Your performance should lead your supervisor to feel informed and confident in you as an attorney. Your goal is to be well organized and to keep the audience on track.

Provide an Introduction and Orienting Information

Begin with the purpose and orienting information, including the roadmap. Starting here provides a structure for the meeting, which is helpful to a listener. With a purpose in mind, the listener can start to immediately contextualize the details you give. With context, your supervisor is less likely to feel frustrated or confused about what you're talking about.

Also, this allows your supervisor to hone or refine the scope, if necessary. For example, your supervisor might need a more abbreviated meeting than you planned for or might be aware of some aspect of the project that you had planned to cover. Remain flexible and allow your supervisor to hone the scope and purpose in real time.

Now that you and your supervisor are clear about the purpose and scope of the meeting, you can proceed with confidence that your supervisor will understand the big picture, which is essential.

Stick Clearly to the Framework

A listener will be doing a constant mental puzzle as you are talking—looking for where, in the big picture, the new information fits. If you're doing a good job, the puzzling will be effortless and mostly subconscious. If not, your audience will likely show signs of frustration. A listener's frustration often comes from a lack of clarity about the structure, not a failure to understand substance. Thus, creating the links to the big picture at regular intervals and at topical shifts is essential to keeping your audience on track and fully informed.

A listener is relying on you to keep him oriented. Provide regular reminders like "that question relates to the second element requiring intent" or "this next provision was added to address the client's desire to limit subleasing." These simple but essential orienting comments help the listener stay on track.

Also, look for clues that your listener has gotten lost: questions or body language that show confusion or frustration. When you see anything that indicates this, return immediately to the framework and provide orienting information.

To best keep a listener oriented, keep the following in mind:

- Use your introduction to provide a roadmap and structure for the discussion.

- Stick to that structure clearly by referencing it while you are talking.

- Use consistent terms and names; name or number points or elements so that you can refer to them quickly and easily.

- Only discuss relevant facts, law, concepts, or ideas. Leave the collateral issues for another time or for the end of the discussion.

Be Open to Discussion and Questions

The meeting is an opportunity for everyone in the room to get on the same page. Allowing space and time for questions and discussion helps ensure that the listener understands what you've explained.

Use Materials and Visuals, If Helpful

Bring helpful materials with you for reference or to help you answer questions you might get. For example, you might bring the most relevant cases (preferably highlighting the important sections) that support you or the case that most worries you. Or you might bring the statute or contract provision that governs your circumstances. But, do not bring everything. It will not likely be convenient or even possible to find a relevant document from the entire file.

And if a visual will help the audience understand a concept or to see the big picture, use it. If a chart or graph helped you understand the issues, it might also be useful to the audience. However, superfluous or unnecessary materials will not impress.

Communication Skills

You're ready: you know your purpose, you have prepared the substance, and you know how to lead an informative meeting. So, now let's consider your delivery and style.

Don't confuse formality for professionalism; a meeting where you are prepared, organized, and professional does not have to be stodgy. In fact, effective communicators are often perceived as relaxed and informal. So, you can and should treat the meeting as a conversation. Don't take this to mean you should kick off your shoes, but relax and have a casual discussion.

The following are some tips to consider for a comfortable and effective communication style for a status meeting.

1. *Create a conversation.* The tone should be pleasant and conversational; it is not a lecture or a speech. Speak clearly and slowly, without sounding unnatural or forced. Avoid reading from notes, a draft, or even a final product. Only refer to documents when necessary, for example, to quote a provision, find a case name, or provide an example.

2. *Remain professional.* Although the meeting can be relaxed, it is still a professional conversation in a professional environment. Err on the side of a more formal, respectful tone. As a general rule, overly casual language, like slang, jargon, and colloquialisms, is not appropriate. And avoid humor (especially inappropriate humor).

3. *Take the lead.* You are the expert and you will be expected to guide the conversation. So, don't expect to be interrupted like a casual conversation, and don't pose questions or look for your supervisor to take over.

4. *Read the room.* Be observant and flexible. Body language and tone of questions can tell you a lot about the audience—is she bored, is he understanding you, does she think you are telling her useless or complicated things? Listen carefully and watch closely to get a feel for what the audience needs—adjust accordingly.

5. *Listen carefully to questions.* Assume the listener is trying to understand, and be responsive. Answer the question asked when it is asked; don't put the question off or delay the answer, even if the question is not relevant. Instead, answer the question or politely explain why it's not relevant. After answering, explain where that subject fits into the bigger picture and continue.

6. *Use plain language.* Use precise, concrete, and easy to understand words and sentences. Do not distract with legalism, big words, or complicated concepts— far from impressing your audience, you will instead bore them, and will seem less informed and less prepared.

7. *Be aware of non-verbal communication.* Your body language and physical appearance communicates a lot about your professionalism and confidence. Be aware of the message you are sending with your posture, your attire, your hand movements, your general demeanor, even your hair style and choice of briefcase. To create the impression of professionalism and confidence, maintain eye contact, sit up straight, limit hand gestures and verbal ticks, and speak at a relaxed pace. Also, make conscious and conservative choices about your personal style: your

clothing, adornments, and accessories send messages. Be in charge of what those messages are.

Summary

No matter what department you work for, a supervisor is likely to ask you for an update at some point. Plan accordingly and remember a few key points:

- It may have a casual tone, but it is a professional and substantive meeting.
- For this meeting, you are the expert.
- Prepare effectively. Know your purpose, the authority, and the structure of the meeting.
- Create a detailed substantive outline as a guide for the meeting.
- Treat this as a conversation but expect to do the talking.
- Be confident in your position. Speak clearly and slowly, without sounding unnatural or forced.
- Relax and create a conversational tone.

Chapter 11

Working Successfully with Secretaries, Paralegals, and Other Staff

Esther Chang[*]

As a first year associate, in addition to learning how to work successfully with your clients, whether those clients are your firm's partners, its senior associates, or its clients, you will also need to learn how to work successfully with the firm's secretaries, paralegals, and other staff. You might think that working successfully with these co-workers is intuitive and therefore easy to do, but many a first year associate has fumbled in the development of these essential working relationships. The results have mitigated the success those first year associates might otherwise have been able to achieve.

---

[*]   Associate, Mayer Brown LLP.

Why Does Successfully Working with Secretaries, Paralegals, and Other Staff Matter?

You might be thinking, why does it matter how successful I am working with my firm's secretaries, paralegals, and other staff, and how could it be anything other than intuitive? They are there to work for me and so long as they do as I ask, we will all be successful. And while that response doesn't sound all that counter-intuitive, you would be missing out on some key insights by viewing your co-workers in such a binary way and by taking this approach toward the development of your working relationship with your firm's secretaries, paralegals, and other staff. Many of you will not have had much prior experience working with secretaries, paralegals, and other staff. Your legal job may very well be your very first "real" job. Even if you were a summer associate at your firm, you probably have not yet had much interaction with your firm's secretaries, paralegals, and other staff. You therefore will not necessarily have come to understand and appreciate the importance of the roles that they play at your firm, and in turn, how important it is that you learn how to work successfully with them for your mutual success.

Your firm's secretaries, paralegals, and other staff can help you improve your efficiency at the firm. Without them, it will take you longer to complete your research, or draft and revise a brief, memo, motion, or contract. Additionally, many of the secretaries, paralegals, and other staff will have been at your firm for years and will have successfully navigated their own careers there. They, in turn, will be able to assist you with navigating the firm's processes, knowing a partner's preferences, and even deciphering a partner's challenging handwriting. They will also take as much administrative work off your hands as you can effectively delegate to them, leaving you to focus on the quality and timeliness of your work product.

Additionally, as a first year associate, you will find that your firm's paralegals are very knowledgeable. While you may not have ever filed a brief, formed a legal entity, or prepared a resolution to be signed by the board of directors of a company, they will have successfully completed all of those assignments. With the assistance of your firm's secretaries, paralegals, and other staff, you will have more time to develop your skill set and to complete your assignments in a timely and efficient matter, with less time and effort devoted to completing other necessary but delegatable tasks.

Good working relationships with your firm's secretaries, paralegals, and other staff will also provide a solid foundation on which to build working relationships with your firm's partners, associates, and clients. Partners and other associates will observe how you interact with the secretaries, paralegals, and other staff, and will also provide feedback about your interactions with them. If any secretary, paralegal, or other staff member is unwilling to work with you, your success at your firm will be negatively impacted. You may find yourself with fewer assignments and a smaller number of partners and associates who are willing to work with you. After all, you are the new member of the firm, and once a team has been developed, if any member is unwilling to work with you, it will be harder to add you as a member of that team.

Hopefully, with just a few examples, you have been convinced that your firm's secretaries, paralegals, and other staff are important to your own success at the firm. If not, perhaps it would help to consider how much more you would have to work if they weren't there to assist you, and whether you would want to also take on the tasks that the secretaries, paralegals and other staff are willing to take off your hands. While such assignments are certainly in their job description, consider how beneficial it is to you as a first year associate that these resources are available to you.

How to Successfully Work with Firm Staff

The "golden rule" is a great way to start. Treat the secretaries, paralegals, and other staff at your firm as you would want to be treated if you were in their shoes.

Treat your co-workers with the respect that you hope will be afforded to you as an associate. As a law student, you will have heard legends about the "screamers" at law firms. You probably cringed when you thought of that happening to you. Likewise, your co-workers probably also cringe at the idea that the lawyers they work for, including you, might do the same to them. Even when you are working under tight timelines and putting in long hours, you must treat co-workers respectfully, because even the intense pressure you may feel you are under is no excuse not to do so.

Carefully consider assignments before delegating. Just as you would prefer to be given an assignment that has been well thought out, with clear instructions as to how to proceed, take the time to do the same when you delegate an assignment to a secretary, paralegal, or other staff. When you have a task that you would like assistance with, consider the following:

- Is this an appropriate task to delegate to your secretary, a paralegal, or other staff (i.e., does this task fall within his or her job description, or should the assignment be completed by someone else)?

- What will the task entail? Does it require some research? Is there a form to fill out?

- Has this task been completed before and is there a sample that may be used as a guideline?

- How long should it take to complete the assignment? When do you need the assignment completed? How much advance notice are you able to provide?
- What else is the person handling at the same time, and how can you resolve competing deadlines?

Taking the time to consider your assignment before delegating it will provide you with the opportunity to determine the best person for the assignment, to provide clear instructions, and to confirm the timing and the work product that you will expect to receive.

Address concerns as they arise. Don't wait for the end of the year to provide feedback in an annual review. Each assignment is a learning opportunity for both you and the person to whom you delegated. Discussing issues as they arise, in a respectful manner, will provide an opportunity for the secretary, paralegal, or other staff member to change the behavior or provide a different and improved work product in the short-term, rather than learning about the negative feedback perhaps much later on.

Ask for feedback. This is also an opportunity to learn how effectively you are communicating, what information the secretary, paralegal, or other staff may need from you in order to accomplish an assignment, and what else you may need to consider in delegating an assignment. The result will more likely be a better work product, which not only helps the staff member at your firm to succeed, but will also reflect positively on you as the work provider.

Try not to micromanage the assignments that you delegate. Just as you would probably find it ineffective and inefficient to be micromanaged by your work providers, try not to micromanage the assignments you delegate to others. Provide clear instructions, but try not to manage every step of the task. Not only is it aggravating to be micromanaged, it is not the most efficient path toward the completion of the client's requested work product. If it will take you as long to explain the assignment as it would to complete the assignment, consider whether the assignment is being appropriately delegated.

Key Takeaways

As a first year associate, you will learn how to navigate the process of working both with the partners, senior associates and clients, and also the secretaries, paralegals, and other staff at your firm. Just as partners, senior associates, and clients will require your assistance, you will require the assistance of your firm's secretaries, paralegals, and other staff—and their assistance is no less valuable than yours. Treat the secretaries, paralegals, and other staff as you would hope to be treated.

Chapter 12

Start to Establish Yourself As a Practice Group or Office Leader

Esther Chang[*]

It Is Never Too Early to Start Raising Your Profile As a Leader

As the newest lawyer on the block, the furthest thing from your mind might be how you can become a leader within your practice group or office. Being a leader might even be a long-term goal of yours, but for now, you may be content with simply being a first year associate, ready and willing to learn from those around you and to excel at being the go-to junior associate for whatever case, project, or transaction walks in the door. Becoming a leader within your practice group or office, however, starts with your first year at the firm. Leaders are not accidentally made. They start right where you are and begin with a decision that someday,

---

[*]   Associate, Mayer Brown LLP.

hopefully in the not too distant future, they want to lead. And if you want to lead, whether it is your practice group or your entire office, make the decision now.

Become a Practice Area Leader

To start, strive to become a leader in your practice area. That means becoming an excellent technical attorney in your chosen area. Read articles and law journals, ask lots of questions, and attend all continuing legal education opportunities to be aware of all developments in your practice. Being a capable, reliable attorney will open many doors to you because leaders in a particular practice area will also be asked to lead others. While it is not always the case that a person with expertise in a particular practice area will also have expertise in leading, practice area expertise is often viewed as a prerequisite to being presented with leadership opportunities. It may take many years for you to become a leader in your practice area, but your initiative to reach this goal and your continued development toward its achievement will not go unnoticed.

The opportunity to write articles and papers or to participate in presentations and lectures will only be made available to those who first demonstrate the substantive expertise required to be a leader in a particular practice area, and only to those who take the initiative to seek out such opportunities. Take each of these opportunities as they are presented to you. They will help you to develop expertise in your practice area and will increase your visibility as a leader in that field.

Participate in Firm Citizenship Roles

You should also seek opportunities to become a leader amongst your peers. From time to time, there will be opportunities to participate in citizenship roles around your firm that will assist with raising your profile as a leader. You may be asked to serve as a mentor for a summer associate, to participate in one of your firm's affinity groups, or to participate in a pro bono activity with other members of your firm. Both seek and take these opportunities. Your willingness to contribute to the success of the firm and your participation will help raise your profile amongst your colleagues, including partners and associates from other practice groups with whom you may not otherwise have an opportunity to work on billable matters.

Treat Colleagues with Respect

Take the time to listen to others. Colleagues may, from time to time, want to discuss with you issues that are important to them. While it may be your first impulse to respond with your opinion, listening more than speaking will provide you with insight into your colleagues' concerns. Over time, you will develop a better understanding as to which concerns are isolated and which concerns are widespread and how such concerns might most effectively be addressed. And once you have that information, be discreet. By being a trusted colleague to your peers, you will earn the respect of everyone.

Celebrate your colleagues' successes and treat your colleagues and their concerns with respect. You can be yourself while also respecting your colleagues' opinions. You will not always agree with one another on issues that are important to your practice group or your firm. Respectfully listen and consider your colleagues' positions.

Conclusion

Developing yourself as a leader in your practice area or office is a long-term goal that starts with your very first day as a first year associate. Your leadership profile will rise throughout your career at the firm as you become an expert in your practice area, demonstrate your willingness to participate in firm citizenship activities, and are seen as a trusted colleague.

Chapter 13

From Draft to Done: Be Your Own Editor

Catharine Du Bois[*]

An essential job of all associates is creating professional work product: written work that does not require substantive editing. Although your supervisors know you are still developing your legal analysis and professional skills, they expect that you will at minimum be able to organize your thoughts into cogent and clear written work free of typographical, syntax, and citation errors. So, it is essential that you quickly learn the art of self-editing.

But editing yourself is very difficult. As the author, you often lack the mental distance necessary to distinguish between what's on the page and what's in your head. When working on a project, you are completely enmeshed in the details; you have a grasp of the minutia that a reader will never have. From this vantage, seeing the missing links and

---

[*] Professor of Legal Research and Writing; Program Director, Writing Persuasive Briefs, National Institute for Trial Advocacy.

understanding what context a reader needs is very difficult. Even seeing proofreading errors is more difficult as an author than as a reader.

Developing a systematic approach for assessing and editing your own work is the best way to find and correct weaknesses and see your work from the reader's eye. And that's what this chapter is about: developing an editing process to see your work as it is, refine it for the benefit of the reader, and produce a professional final product. As Joseph Williams and Joseph Bizup state in their book, *Style: Lessons in Clarity and Grace*, "Most experienced writers like to get something down on paper or up on the screen as fast as they can. Then as they revise that draft into something clearer, they understand their ideas better. And when they understand their ideas better, they express them more clearly, and the more clearly they express them, the better they understand them . . . and so it goes, ending only when they run out of energy, interest, or time."[1]

The Editing Process

The editing process is a way to turn your writer-focused first draft—the draft where you likely wrote your way to understanding the issues—into a reader-focused final—a document written for a reader to easily understand. A systematic editing process helps you focus your attention on identifiable and individual parts of the document so that you can look critically at the overall success as well as the success at every level—from overall flow, to the flow of each section, to each paragraph, to each sentence.

---

1. JOSEPH M. WILLIAMS & JOSEPH BIZUP, STYLE: LESSONS IN CLARITY AND GRACE (12th ed. 2017), at 7.

But most writers don't have a process; instead, they "wing it." The result is unorganized and undirected and often involves merely reading over the document looking for proofreading and syntax errors and hoping that, by fixing those, the organizational problems and logical inconsistencies will correct themselves. They won't.

Although editing includes proofreading and polishing, editing is more than just that. Editing also tests the document to make sure that the question is answered, the purpose is clear, the logic is sound, the structure is obvious, and the theme is cohesive. And an effective process identifies different levels of review and creates a systematic approach. To maximize efficiency, start with the big picture aspects like overall purpose, structure, and content. Then, when you are confident in the big picture, move on to review at the next level, ending with word choice and sentence structure and finally, proofreading and format.

Although an effective process can be broken into as many stages as you wish, this chapter identifies four main editing stages.

General Editing Tips

Before discussing the individual stages, there are a few things that apply to editing in general. While editing, keep in mind these suggestions for a more effective and efficient process:

- **Take time away from the text.** Put the draft away for a while; clear your head of what you think you've written so you can take a fresh look and see what is really on the page.

- **Edit on paper.** Review and make notes on a hard copy. This helps you get distance from the draft and also increases efficiency by reducing the impulse to correct in real time. If you are worried about wasting paper, print double-sided and be sure to recycle. You will waste more paper by having a partner go through more revisions later if you poorly edit in the early stages.

- **Don't correct immediately.** Finish each review completely before editing. This helps you get a full picture of what needs to be addressed before trying to fix any one piece or any individual error. And this helps ensure that you will devote as much time to the final pages as you do to the first ones.

- **Watch for patterns.** Knowing what kind of problems you have will be helpful in adapting your editing process. Once you have identified a pattern, you can develop techniques for spotting and correcting the problem. For example, if you notice that your paragraphs often cover multiple distinct concepts rather than one single idea, you can create an editing step that reviews each paragraph.

- **Refining and rewriting.** As you work through each stage, you will find aspects or concepts that either were missing or were unnecessary, and you will need to refine and rewrite. Earlier stages might require substantial redrafting and editing and sometimes even additional research. After completing edits, repeat the stage until you are confident that the draft is ready for the next level of review.

The Stages of Editing Your Work

Stage 1: The Big Picture

At this stage, you are assessing the draft at a bird's-eye view, looking for the purpose, the overall content, and the structure. This is the time to make sure that you've actually done what you set out to do and to confirm that everything you've included is necessary and that nothing is missing.

Purpose

First identify the purpose (or goal) of the document. The assignment asked you to do something specific: write an argument, research a question, draft or edit an agreement, summarize a client meeting. Does the draft do what you were asked to do?

Once you are clear about the purpose of the assignment, review your draft to confirm that the draft serves that purpose throughout.

Practice Tip: An effective way—and often a welcome way—to make sure you're on track is to go back to the assigning attorney with an outline. Schedule a very short "touch base" meeting. Present a clear and concise outline of (1) what you understood the assignment to be and (2) what you're planning to write up. This gives the assigning attorney an opportunity to confirm the assignment and to refine it, if necessary. This can also be accomplished via email, but a face-to-face meeting is often more effective and efficient. (And, it's a great way to build rapport with your supervisors.)

Content

Once you've confirmed the purpose, check the content to make sure that everything you've included serves that purpose consistently and logically. Review for missing links, for irrelevant or off-topic sections, and for things that detract from the overall message. Confirm that the claims and conclusion you make are accurate and supported, that the argument is logical and persuasive. Delete or move anything that isn't necessary to serve the purpose, and note where information is missing.

Structure

Finally, assess the organization and confirm that the framework is logical and clear. Catherine Cameron and Lance Long note, "One of the greatest efforts you can make in your writing to increase reader comprehension is to give your reader a sense of organization to the material you are presenting. . . . [T]his emphasis on demonstrating a structure for the reader is supported by studies of cognitive psychologists . . . that showed these structural components can have a positive effect on learning and reader comprehension."[2]

The structure of a document provides essential information to the reader. It gives the reader a frame of reference and a sense of what's to come, both of which are essential to comprehension.

---

2.   Catherine J. Cameron & Lance N. Long, The Science Behind the Art of Legal Writing (2015), at 79.

Stage 2: Context and Internal Organization

At this stage, you are working with a well-organized draft that is on point and has the necessary elements to be successful. So it's time to take a closer look. Here, you will be assessing whether the document provides the necessary context and looking at the organization of each section.

Context

Readers need to be oriented with effective context and background information before they can understand and make sense of the details. Orienting information includes the purpose of the document, a roadmap that describes the structure of the document, and the background facts and relevant authority. No matter the kind of document, orienting information is essential to reader comprehension. For example, a brief might include background facts, procedural history, and the legal framework; a contract might include definitions, parties, and goals; and a letter or email might open with an explanation of the reason for writing.

Review the document to make sure that the necessary context is there and that it is clear.

Internal Organization

Next, look at each section of the document to make sure that the flow is logical and follows a clear progression. Confirm that the progression of ideas makes sense and that it builds logically, moving from the broad concepts to the more detailed concepts.

Create a topic sentence outline to test logical flow. The topic sentence is the first sentence of each paragraph and it should reflect the content of the paragraph. By looking at only the topic sentences, you should be able to understand the structure. If you read only the topic sentences of a well-written memo, brief, letter, even an email, you will have a very clear picture of the content of the document.

The opposite is true of a poorly written document. And readers know this. Some know to scan topic sentences first, looking for clear structure. If the topic sentences aren't strong and don't outline an obvious progression of ideas, the reader knows that the document is going to be weak. Other readers may not consciously be aware that the topic sentences aren't strong but will nevertheless feel lost and confused by the document if the topic sentences are weak and do not reflect a logical flow.

Mastering strong topic sentences for everything you write, from emails to briefs to executive summaries, can be the first step to dramatically improving your writing.

It is definitely worth the initial time and attention that focusing on topic sentences requires.

Here's the logic:

- *If* your topic sentences are thesis statements,
- *If* they clearly articulate the structure of the logic of your document, and
- *If* the content of each paragraph actually supports the topic sentence fully,
- *Then* your document is perfectly organized.

That's worth saying again: perfectly organized. That's how transformative mastering topic sentences can be.

Stage 3: Paragraphs and Sentences

In this final content review, you are looking even more closely at the flow of ideas within individual paragraphs, between sentences, and within sentences.

Paragraph Content and Structure

Let's return to the topic sentences. By reviewing the topic sentences in the previous stage, you confirmed that the progression of paragraphs follows a logical flow. Now it's time to look at the sentences within each paragraph to make sure each sentence completely and logically supports the topic sentence.

The content of each paragraph should be limited to the idea defined by the topic sentence. And the sentences should progress in a logical order, moving from broader concepts to more specific details. Delete or move any sentence that does not help explain or defend the topic sentence. Add any missing links or missing support. And reorganize so that the sentences progress logically.

Sentence Clarity and Style

Once you have confirmed that every sentence is necessary, that nothing is missing, and that the flow is logical, look at each sentence individually. Edit and refine so that your sentences are clear and easy to understand.

Your style and individual writing habits should dictate what you look for in this stage. But below are a few tips for achieving clarity:

- **Use short sentences, especially for complicated thoughts.** Look at sentence construction and adopt a basic subject, verb, object construction as a baseline that you can build on for more dynamic sentences.

- **Use active voice sentence structure and use dynamic informative verbs.**

- **Use simple, plain English.** Avoid the temptation to impress with complex sentence structure or thesaurus words. Far from impressing, it will more likely confuse and frustrate the reader.

- **Use effective transitions between sentences.** Adding a simple transition word or phrase provides essential information about the next idea. For example, simply adding "thus" or "in contrast" to the beginning of a sentence tells the reader what the connection is between the two statements.

- **Use the appropriate tone and style for the document.** For example, are you adopting an appropriately respectful yet persuasive tone for a brief to a court? Have you presented the options objectively and without bias in a summary letter to a client?

- **Remove unnecessary or extra words, including legal phrases.** At least 30% of most first drafts are unnecessary words.

- **Use consistent terms and names.**

Stage 4: Proofreading and Polishing

Proofreading and polishing is the final stage of the editing process, focusing on typographical problems like misspelled or misused words, incorrect sentence syntax, grammar and punctuation errors, and formatting inconsistencies.

Many writers spend only a few minutes proofreading, hoping to catch errors that jump off the page and even believing that typographical errors aren't a big deal. But proofreading errors affect the success of the document. Incorrect sentence structure or even just a missing word can significantly alter the meaning. They distract and can and usually do cause the reader to distrust you as a writer. As retired Supreme Court Justice John Paul Stevens has said, "[I]t's perhaps unfair, but if someone uses improper grammar you begin to think well maybe the person isn't as careful about his or her work as he or she should be."[3]

A quick and cursory reading often misses a lot, especially after you've been working long and hard on something. Developing a process for proofreading can help you tackle the process effectively and efficiently every time.

Your Proofreading Process

Develop a step-by-step process and follow it every time you proofread. This will help you identify and correct more errors in less time. Base your process on your writing needs. As a start, consider the errors you commonly make or the writing style you'd like to develop. For example, if you tend to be wordy, adopt a step that requires you to edit out three to five words per sentence; if you misuse modifiers, adopt a step that finds modifying phrases and confirms that they clearly link to the correct object; or if you know you struggle with comma usage, adopt a step that requires you to mark each comma and confirm that it is correct.

As a bonus, a systematic approach can help you exchange bad habits for good ones. Let's look at an example: imagine that, to target your habit of writing in passive voice, you adopt a system to highlight sentences that begin with "there is," "there are," and "it is," an easily identifiable passive structure. After applying this step consistently, you will likely start to notice your habit while drafting and make a conscious choice to draft differently (since you know you're going to have to correct it later!). Over time, the conscious choice will become a matter of routine. And in short order,

---

3. *See Interviews with United States Supreme Court Justices*, THE SCRIBES JOURNAL OF LEGAL WRITING, at 49 (2010), http://legaltimes. typepad.com/files/garner-transcripts-1.pdf.

you will have created a new good habit, resulting in a stronger drafting style.

The following tips can help you create your own proofreading process:

- **Change the way the document looks.** By changing the text size, spacing, or style and by altering margins or line spacing, you trick your brain into thinking it's seeing an unfamiliar document, helping you see the document as a reader, not the author.

- **Chunk.** Limiting your review to a single section can make the process seem more manageable. When it feels manageable, you will be more likely to devote your attention fully and will find more errors more efficiently.

- **Do one thing at a time.** If you try to correct too many kinds of errors at the same time, you risk losing focus. You are more likely to catch grammar errors if you aren't checking punctuation and spelling at the same time. In addition, some of the techniques that work well for spotting one kind of mistake won't catch others.

- **Read out loud.** You will catch missing words, long complicated sentences, hard to understand concepts, and awkwardly worded phrases more easily when you read them aloud. If you can't say it clearly and easily, your reader can't read it that way.

- **Read backward.** Read each sentence in reverse order from the end to the beginning. Read each sentence separately, looking for grammar, punctuation, or spelling errors. This does a couple of things: (1) it helps you read for errors in each sentence without getting distracted by the flow of the paragraph and

(2) it helps you focus on the end with as much attention as you focus on the beginning.

- **Use (but don't rely on) computer tools.** Word processing tools can be useful, but they are far from foolproof. For example, spell checkers will not catch misspellings that form another valid word, like "there" when you meant "their." And, grammar checkers rely on limited rules, so they can't identify every error and often make mistakes. Use them to assist you, but do not let them do the work for you.

- **Check every punctuation mark.** This forces you to look at each one. Confirm that each mark is correct. Punctuation rules are specific and are learnable; the rules are not optional or based on personal preference. Don't guess about how to properly use punctuation.

- **Use reference books and resources.** You're not just looking for errors that you recognize; you're also learning to recognize and correct new errors. So, keep helpful resources close at hand as you proofread. And if you're not sure about something, look it up. (By the way, a reference tool does not have to be a book. Grammar and usage websites can be very good. But pick a reputable source.)

Formatting

The final thing to do before calling it done is look at the way the text falls on the page. Make sure that the formatting is consistent and looks professional. Headings, margins, paragraph indents and spacing, line spacing, page breaks, and page numbers are all places where inconsistency or carelessness can affect overall impressions.

Summary

Developing the skill of editing your own work is an essential part of being an associate. Your supervisors and colleagues expect well-organized and perfectly proofread work. Editing your own work is more efficient and effective when you develop a process that helps you see your work from a reader's perspective. Be a strong editor by developing a process that addresses your strengths and weaknesses and one that you can adapt as your drafting skills and habits change.

Chapter 14

Own Your Career

Annapoorni Sankaran[*]

If you are anything like most new large firm associates, you just finished law school and you have your fair share of student loans. If you have not yet paid off your degree, how are you expected to own your career already?

Currently, I am a minority woman partner at a large global law firm. However, I grew up with Indian parents—so to them, if I was not going to be a doctor, I might as well have become a meth addict. I am one of only two attorneys in my family and I had no experience about what it took to get into law school, how to be successful in school, how to seek and find a legal job (let alone a career), and how to create my success. But, I was hell-bent on proving to my family and community that the law is an important profession that was intellectual and allowed me to help others. Most of all, I wanted them to know that immigrants could be successful at this honorable profession.

What I learned was that my career is my business, and I am the CEO of that business. You are not just a bystander

---

[*]   Partner, Holland & Knight LLP.

in this career you have chosen. Now it is time to create your business plan. Although it may sound daunting, it is also an amazing next path on which you are about to embark. It is the time to take ownership of the success of your business and plan for your achievements. Below are some tools to help you make your journey more successful.

Find Mentors

One of the best things to do in your career—and that I still do to this day—is to find a mentor. Not just one—many over time. Like purses and shoes, you need many styles to help you adapt and flourish in each situation. You will have mentors who help you with your substantive skills to be a talented lawyer. Other mentors will help you be your best at social functions—meeting people, making connections, and expanding and using your network. Other mentors will teach you about community service. These mentors will help you find a passion and give back to your community in ways that resonate with you. If your mentors are good, they will not always tell you how wonderful you are, but will teach you some of the difficult lessons. In each of their own ways, your mentors will help you navigate and advance through your career.

How do you find the right mentor? Stop and listen. Find people who do things that matter to you. If you like how someone treated another lawyer, or if you admire how someone negotiated bringing in a new client, or if someone argues an amazing appeal—ask them about it, learn from it, and take the skills that feel like you. Everything about being a successful lawyer is about being authentic and true to your personality and brand.

My first mentor was a partner at my firm. I did most of my work for him. He was a yeller and a screamer. I went home every day in tears but happy I was not fired. Eventually, I won him over. He saw me as an intellectual powerhouse when I dissected a complex legal issue. He tried calling me out with what he thought was a difficult question about which I had not thought. But I had the answer and truly impressed him. I forever won his respect. When I had the opportunity to bring in my first client as an associate, he helped me navigate that process and made sure that I got due credit in the firm. He was proud of me and supported me. He held me to the highest standards; and the technical litigation skills I have are due to his mentorship.

One of the other things I have done to find mentors is identify successful women both in my firm and in the community. I then reached out to them and set up meetings. In those meetings, I simply asked them to tell me their story of how they got to where they are. I have met some exceptional people who now also have invested in my success. But more importantly, when I listened to each of their stories, I learned the techniques they used to be successful when they found themselves in certain situations in which I also found myself. I used those tools and techniques to help elevate my career.

Getting the most out of the mentoring relationship is largely your responsibility. Do not rely on your mentor to identify your strengths and weaknesses and give you advice regarding each. Also keep in mind that the mentor that gets assigned to you may not always be the perfect fit. Be mindful of the fact that your mentors are busy professionals, and although they have your best interests at heart, they will not always be focused on you. You need to regularly ask for specific feedback and advice. And, when you need a new mentor for some reason—you want to learn some different skills, you need someone with experience to help you with a specific situation, or the fit is just not right—go find one. By owning the relationship, you can own your success.

Define and Establish Your Brand

What kind of lawyer do you want to be? What are the descriptors you want to conjure about your abilities when people mention your name? Think about your brand. You want people to want to work with you. Every interaction you have defines that. So, make sure you sweat the small stuff and let people know that you care about the details. Never miss a deadline; proofread immaculately; and know what is going on in your supervisor's schedule.

Treat every assignment like you were briefing to the Supreme Court and put your highest quality work product out there. Do not give in to any temptations to take short-cuts. Treat people with respect and kindness. You know the impression that people make who treat a waiter or waitress poorly? That is the same thing you do by "talking down" to office or court staff. Treat everyone how you would want your parents to be treated. Take the time to listen and learn from every situation—things you could have done better, or repeat challenges your clients encounter.

All of your experiences will weave together to help you form critical judgment and decision-making skills necessary to advise your clients. Make and use your network. The more people you know, the more connections you have to assist others. Appreciate people's differences and the value it adds to your workplace. When things go wrong, how you treat people and how you solve problems reflect on your character and the skills and demeanor you bring to the table. In defining your brand, decide whether you want to be Atticus Finch or Vinny Gambini.

Learn the Business of Law and the Business of Your Clients

To be a good CEO, you need to know your business inside and out. There is more to the law than negotiating the best deal or winning a trial. Law firms are businesses. Each lawyer and staff member is essential to the functioning of that business. Take the time to learn about yours and how you fit into it. Learn about the financial metrics that determine whether your firm is profitable. What kind of overhead does your firm have (rent, benefits, technology, etc.)? How much income do you need to generate so that the firm breaks even in employing you? Who are your firm's competitors? How do the lawyers in the office generate business? What goes into getting a new client? What goes into keeping a client? What do the bills that the clients see look like? Learning all of these aspects will help you understand how you fit into the big picture. Having that understanding will allow you to find where your talents lie and create opportunities for you to add value to the firm.

In that same way, learn about the business of your clients so you can understand their motivations and culture. Who is the person who gives your law firm direction? Where does he or she fit into his or her corporate structure? What makes that person look good to his/her boss? What is going on in your client's industry? Does the business or industry have any economic challenges? What is the structure of your client's financing? Is your client a public or private company? Is it family owned? Learn who the people are at your client and where they are in their careers. In-house attorneys and executives repeatedly report that they pick lawyers with whom they have true connections. So, your job is to build those connections as they are essential to the longevity of the relationship both with that individual person and the business. The more you know, the more common points you can find and the more connected you can be. In addition, the more you know about the business and the industry, the better contextual advice you can give to help them achieve their business goals. Any person who can do both of these things is a person who belongs on the team.

Set Annual Goals

All successful businesses set annual goals so that they can focus attention on achieving desirable outcomes. Goals channel your brain toward finding solutions. So, in order to make your business a success, it is important to set annual goals. When creating your list, make sure your goals are very specific. So, a goal like "get better at writing" can be broken down into specific tasks such as: "draft at least one motion to dismiss or a motion for summary judgment," and "take a legal writing continuing legal education course." The goal needs to be something specific you can check off when you finish. Which leads to the next criteria: your goals also need to be measurable and achievable within the year for which you set them.

When you set goals at the beginning of your career, focus on learning and mastering the substantive skills of your practice area. Use the resources in your office to do that, including any professional development resources and other lawyers senior to you. Each year, as you advance, consider adding goals outside strict substantive skills, including: writing, speaking, seeking membership and leadership within various legal and community organizations, and business development. Always make sure to define specific and measurable goals for the year: "attend an ERISA conference," "write an article on a bankruptcy topic," or "bring in one client."

Bring your mentor into this process, at a minimum, on a yearly basis. He or she can help you refine your goals and may suggest new ones of which you did not think. In addition, they can offer you suggestions and introduce you to connections that may help you achieve those goals. They might be able to help you get a speaking role at a conference. Or, let's say that your goal is to work on a class action lawsuit, your mentor might help you navigate how to get on one of those cases.

Once you have defined your goals, let people know about them. The law is a collaborative profession and your superiors want you to be successful. It will be far easier to achieve your goals by using the resources around you to find the opportunities to make them happen. In addition, by making your list public, you hold yourself accountable. Setting specific and measurable annual goals and achieving them will give you control over your success.

Manage Your Reviews

Each year you will get reviewed—the "Annual Report" of your business. You have a lot more control over this process than you think. One of the most important things to consider is that many times in life, perceptions can become reality, especially in the review process. When I was a mid-level associate, I received my annual review and was told by one of the partners, "You have not worked on any major cases this year and you have not written any substantive briefs." But the reality was that I had done both of these things; he just did not know it. And once it hit my written review, that misperception became the firm's reality about me. So here are some steps to avoid this situation, and more importantly, take control over the review process so that it can be a positive building block for your advancement and compensation.

At the beginning of your year, ask your supervisors what their goals are for you and what they want you to work on. A week or so before your superiors fill out their reviews about you, give them a one-page memo that lists your hours, generations, the goals they identified for you, what you did to achieve them, notable matters or projects on which you worked, any of your business development, and your community involvement. This gives them a one-stop tool that will help them better fill out your review. Notably, too, by doing this, you have a voice in creating the narrative that forms your "Annual Report."

When you have your actual review, make sure you ask where you are succeeding, where they would like to see you improve, and any specific goals they would like you to accomplish in the future. Make sure you write all of that down so that you can use that information for the next year. Then, repeat!

Push Yourself Outside Your Comfort Zone

We all get used to certain routines and stay within them. That is because it is safe, there is predictability, and risk is at a minimum. We have a good idea of what will happen when we stay with what is comfortable and we know. Being comfortable is not a bad thing. As lawyers, our jobs are to identify and minimize risk. But comfortable routines can lead to complacency. Challenging yourself will help you reach peak performance levels. In addition, trying new things will help you meet new people, including people who would normally fall within your social circles. This expanding network will bring diversity of thought into your life as well as a larger group of people to help and from whom you can draw. Taking risks will help you learn about your strengths and weaknesses, and importantly, will help you build self-confidence. By forcing yourself to tackle the unknown, you will also gain the skills, judgment, and wisdom to handle the unpredictable world in which we live.

Think about what might be uncomfortable to you and set a goal to try one of those things. Maybe it is running a half marathon, speaking at a conference, tennis, writing a blog, archery, or anything else. Pick one each year and make a New Year's resolution to give it a try. Personally, I have tried modeling, spin class, parkour, karaoke, stand-up comedy, and acting, to name a few. I have learned a lot about myself as a result, made a lot of invaluable friends, and found new business. Change is a good thing; it opens doors and helps you fashion creative solutions to reach your maximum potential.

After years of school, lots of examinations, and lots of money spent, you have now entered a very honorable profession. Honor that investment and focus on what you want your business to be. You have the power to define the terms so take some time to think about how you would like this experience to be. You will need to make changes and adapt to the situations that life hands you. But most importantly, you will have the tools to have a successful journey.

Chapter 15

Self-Care for the First Year

Anne Collier[*]

It's so exciting! You're starting your first year at Awesome Law, and you are teetering between elation and terror. Terror might be an exaggeration, but not much of one. You summered at Awesome Law and know it's the right place for you. Yet, you are concerned that you might blow it. You want to make sure that you have a great first year, and that stress doesn't derail your success or relationships. You want to hit the ground running yet know you're at the beginning of a marathon. How can you maximize the opportunity to become a great lawyer and someone that colleagues and clients respect and rely on?

One critical step in this exciting, fulfilling, and sometimes exasperating journey is learning how to manage your behavior under stress, thus becoming more resilient and less reactive. Resilience is the ability to recover quickly from

---

[*] Founder and CEO, Arudia.

difficulties. Being less reactive means that you choose how to respond; you do not let your stress or fear unwittingly drive your behavior. As you can imagine, the latter is unproductive and can damage a career.

It also means maintaining a steady state of emotional health and well-being as well as avoiding what Daniel Goleman refers to as the "Amygdala Hijack."[1] The amygdala is the part of our brain that handles emotions and responds to a threat with fight, flight, freeze, or appease. The Amygdala Hijack is an immediate and overwhelming emotional response out of proportion to the stimulus because it has triggered a more significant emotional threat.[2] If you don't manage your body's response to potentially stressful stimuli, your reaction to the stimuli takes over, itself becoming an obstacle to dealing effectively with the situation.

Your reaction to threatening stimuli, such as a looming deadline or, worse yet, many deadlines, can be overwhelming. You may feel like something is being *done to you*. But don't lose sight of the truth: you are your body and mind, and stress is something *you do* in response to stimuli. While it can be a struggle to stop the mind and body from reacting to a looming deadline as if it were a snarling predator, you can develop strategies for avoiding the Amygdala Hijack and chronic stress.

The consequences of failing to manage stress are clear. Examples of the effects of short-term stress include knotted shoulders, a racing or distracted mind, and short or explosive remarks that damage relationships with people who matter, including oneself. As stress becomes chronic, it erodes the body's ability to prevent illness and heal, con-

---

1. DANIEL GOLEMAN, EMOTIONAL INTELLIGENCE: WHY IT CAN MATTER MORE THAN IQ (New York: Bantam Books 1996).
2. *Id.*

tributing to asthma, back pain, gastrointestinal disorders, and heart disease.[3] Chronic stress can also lead to depression, pervasive unease, and impair judgments, perceptions, and overall cognitive function.

The good news is that you can have a great career and avoid burnout if you identify and implement strategies that:

1. Create an empowering self-care regime;

2. Heighten your self-awareness;

3. Improve overall resilience and reduce reactivity; and

4. Short-circuit stress before reacting to it.

Adopting a few of the strategies described herein will increase your overall sense of well-being and calm, and will allow you to more effectively prioritize, focus, and follow through so that you have a great first year practicing law.

Create an Empowering Self-Care Regime

When you're in your mid-twenties, you may not appreciate the importance of the basics such as getting enough sleep, eating right, and exercising. This is not out-of-date advice from your mother. Nor is it advice geared to a pudgy forty-year-old. It's advice for you. To learn and excel, you must take care of your body, which will result in you having more energy and the ability to think and learn.

Sleep. Let's start with sleep. While it may seem obvious, depriving yourself of sleep has negative consequences. And yet, so many people regularly fail to get adequate sleep. Remember, you have chosen a career in which *your brain*

---

3. American Psychological Association, *Stress effects on the body* (2016), http://www.apa.org/helpcenter/stress-body.aspx (last visited June 13, 2018).

power is the key to your success. And yet, when you don't sleep, you suffer cognitive impairment, and you are forgetful and easily distracted. Moreover, your perceptions and judgment become compromised. You think more slowly. Not characteristics of a superstar lawyer; not you! Learn to be realistic about what you can commit to and don't over-schedule yourself. Remember that colleagues are forming opinions of you in your first year, and you want those opinions to help, not haunt, you.

Eat. In addition to sleep, you need to eat right and avoid drinking too much alcohol, especially during the week. Again, this may sound like your mother's advice, but she knows a thing or two! Think about food as fuel. You wouldn't expect your car to run well on polluted fuel, would you? Or on an empty tank? Be sure to get enough protein and healthy fats to ensure that your brain is both assimilating the facts and the law and producing great written work. Also, avoid sugar, especially on an empty stomach. This is because eating sugar on an empty stomach gives you the rush, followed by the crash. The crash doesn't support great work, relaxation, or the enjoyment of friends and family. So, what are you to do if you don't have anyone packing lunch or snacks for you? Here's what some lawyers do:

- Lunch out with a colleague most days; this improves integration into the firm while providing the needed mental break.

- If eating out, make healthy choices at lunch, or pack a simple lunch and snacks that include a lot of protein, such as leftovers from dinner, hard-boiled eggs, or nut butters.

- Use lunch to get a short walk in, which provides the needed mental break and exercise to and from a favorite take-out spot.

Exercise. Now that you are working, sleeping, and eating right, there can't possibly be enough time to exercise, right? Wrong! Even if you aren't driven to exercise, you need exercise to clear your mind, think clearly, and to take care of your body. Exercise can include yoga, weight training, running, cycling, or simply walking. In fact, lawyers who find a way to include exercise as a by-product of another activity, such as part of a commute, don't struggle to find time to exercise.

Managing It All. You ask the practical question, "How do I get enough sleep, eat right, exercise, work hard, and have a personal life?" This is when you take a step back and make some empowering and powerful choices about work-life integration. The irony is that to enjoy your legal career, you must work hard. This is because investing time in your legal career is how you learn and experience "flow," which occurs when you are so engrossed in your work that you lose track of time. That said, you also must recognize when continuing to work won't be productive, and that it would be more effective to get some sleep and resume in the morning. You'll likely want to use weekends to catch up or get ahead on the parts of life that may be a little out of balance.

A secret to achieving successful work-life integration is to develop routines that support you in being sharp and ready to work while you enjoy time with family and friends. Why routines? Because when activities are part of a routine, you don't have to think about them. They just occur. You don't ponder whether to brush your teeth in the morning or evening, do you? Of course not, you just do it. Think about these routines as being like an automatic sprinkler system that turns on for fifteen minutes every morning at 4 a.m., without you having to think about it. Examples include:

- A senior associate who decided that she wouldn't give up working out and does so faithfully every morning. She also routinely stays late Monday and Thursday nights to get a jump on work.

- One associate plays softball Saturday mornings and works out after work two other days during the week.

- An associate who is a parent walks his children to school every morning on the way to the train, leaves work promptly at 5 p.m., and typically works after dinner three nights a week.

While there is no secret formula, the secret *is to have a formula.*

Heighten Your Self-Awareness

The Amygdala Hijack is as awful as it sounds. It's when the reptilian part of your brain takes over. You are reactive. It's those times when you are not yourself; you are in fight, flight, freeze, or appease mode. Not only is it an overwhelming, negative experience for you, but it's also awful for those around you and, consequently, is not career-enhancing. So, how do you avoid the Amygdala Hijack?

Perhaps most important is improving your self-awareness to better manage yourself. It means truly knowing how to maximize your strengths and minimize the effects of your blind spots, which includes knowing what causes you to respond to stress in an unproductive manner. Personality assessments are quite useful in this regard. Learning your Myers-Briggs Type® (referred to as "Type") is not just interesting, but extremely useful, because it helps you focus on maximizing your natural strengths while mitigating the effects of blind spots. We all have blind spots, meaning that we all encounter certain tasks that are difficult, require a lot of focus, and are, consequently, stressful in large doses. Rather than becoming frustrated and engaging in self-flagellation, you can embrace the blind spots as merely another fact of life—another problem to solve. And, you're a problem solver, right?

Type is a theory of preferences for one of each of the four dichotomies; each person prefers one of each of the following pairs:

- **The Energy Flow Attitude,** which describes the *Extraverted* world of people and activity and the *Introverted* world of reflection;

- **The Perception Functions,** which describe how people perceive information via *Sensing* (details, specifics, and here and now) and *iNtuition* (the meaning of *Sensing* information, patterns, generalities, and future focus);

- **The Judging Functions,** which describe how people analyze and make decisions about the *Sensing* and *iNtuitive* information that they have perceived. *Thinking* describes decision making that is based on logical standards; *Feeling* is based on subjective standards and person-based values; and

- **The Outer-World Attitude,** which describes the use of either one's preferred Judging Function or Perception Function in the outer world. Behaviorally, *Judgers* look scheduled, decided, and systematic; *Perceivers* look more open-minded, go-with-the-flow, and can delay decisions and change their mind as they wait for and obtain more information.

Consider one lawyer's reflection: "I learned about Type and work style. What became clear is that I need a lot of structure—more than most—to be effective. So now I don't feel guilty or stupid taking the time to create structure. I came to appreciate that I need my time alone because I prefer Introversion, which means that I plan time to be alone to think through problems. I used to be a little embarrassed, almost like there was something wrong with me. But now, I figure out how to make the time. I think about when I have to be on and when I can recharge. I also learned that when I am churning my wheels, my Type gets clarity from talking out the issues. The point is that you can manage yourself to be more effective *and* less stressed."

Another benefit of knowing your Type relates specifically to managing stress and the Amygdala Hijack. Each Type has stress triggers and remedies. In addition to setting up automatic-sprinkler systems to get ahead of stress, you'll want to learn how to recognize your triggers so that you can choose to respond in a positive manner, rather than letting your amygdala hijack your thinking. Understanding that you have a choice in how you respond is necessary to managing your behavior under stress.

For example, imagine that you are under pressure and verging on being overwhelmed; you are acting in a manner that is uncharacteristically negative and reflects your Type's pattern of behavior under stress. You trust your perceptions and judgments, and therefore also believe that you are doing what is best, given the circumstances. Guess what? You are not doing what's best. Likely, stress is clouding your judgment—it's running you. Once you realize the impact of the stress on your perceptions, judgments, and behaviors, you'll have the perspective to choose more productive behavior, which means you are less reactive.[4]

So, what is a first year to do? Insight is great and is essential, but how do you improve mental resilience and reduce reactivity? The answer is that, in addition to taking care of yourself, you need to work on confidence, performance, and renewal (next section). You will also need to develop strategies for dealing with stress in the moment (the penultimate section).

Improve Overall Resilience and Reduce Reactivity

The Actualized Leader framework[5] posits that to develop greater resilience and to reduce your reactivity to triggers, you need to improve your confidence, performance, or renewal. To improve confidence, you need to improve your objectivity, courage, and candor. Examples of strategies for improvement include:

- Practice describing situations factually and without judgment. Leave out the adjectives. Notice your assumptions; distinguish both implicit and explicit assumptions from what happened. This will also make you a better lawyer!

- When you need to raise a concern or fess up to a mistake, consider the worst that might happen; is it so bad? What will happen if you don't act? Consider

---

4. For more about Type and stress, see NAOMI L. QUENK, IN THE GRIP: UNDERSTANDING TYPE, STRESS, AND THE INFERIOR FUNCTION (Palo Alto, CA: Consulting Psychologists Press 2000).

5. *See* WILLIAM L. SPARKS, ACTUALIZED LEADERSHIP: MEETING YOUR SHADOW AND MAXIMIZING YOUR POTENTIAL (forthcoming).

what you'd like colleagues and clients to think of you, and which actions further that vision.

- Use neutral, factual language when raising concerns that seem negative or have negative implications.

To improve performance, you need to improve your ability to focus, be trusting of others to follow through, and have more moments of flow. The latter is akin to being *in the zone*. Examples of strategies include:

- Stop kidding yourself: you aren't multi-tasking; you're multi-switching. You may think you can work on more than one task at a time, but you can't. All you are doing is switching between tasks, and likely doing neither very well. Work for fifteen minutes on a project without distraction, then decide if you'll work another fifteen minutes on it or switch to another project.

- Trusting others is a concept applied to those you manage, which is unlikely to occur during your first year. That said, practice making sure that expectations *of you* are clear and set milestones for checking in with more senior lawyers. Soon enough you'll be managing more junior associates, and you'll need to do the same for them.

- Turn off email, your phone, and your computer's volume and work on a project until you're done or out of ideas; switch to the next project and repeat.

To feel more refreshed and renewed, you need to improve your ability to be present, be more accepting of yourself (including perceived flaws), and value solitude. Examples of strategies include:

- Listen to others, focusing on the core message and the person's feelings and needs with respect to a situation. This is good practice for a lawyer at any level!
- When you are distracted by the thought of another task, write it down to remove the distraction, and then continue working.
- It's easy to look at others and wish to be more like them. Choose to view such a comparison as aspirational and inspirational, rather than a sign of inadequacy. Remember that everyone has strengths and blind spots, and all there is to do is accept the blind spots and develop strategies for ensuring they don't derail your success. For example, if you aren't good with details, write everything down. And, choose to enjoy your life, flaws and all.
- Use time to yourself to actively plan, reflect, and renew; engage in an enjoyable activity such as exercise, reading, or cooking.

Learn to Short-Circuit Stress

Finally, even if you've taken all the advice in this chapter, you may still be overwhelmed by stress run amok. You can short-circuit stress to minimize its effect on your well-being and productivity before you are in its grip. Because stress is a non-specific emotion and physical reaction to stimuli, you can short-circuit it by choosing to respond, rather than reacting with fight-or-flight instincts. Using the following three-step process will help you return to effectiveness and productivity:

Step 1: Be Present

Replace tension and clutter with clarity by navigating to now. Take time away from the stressful stimuli.

Physical Time Away

If you can, go for a short walk. If you can't, focus on diminishing the physical symptoms of stress. Try improving the quality of your breathing by inhaling more deeply and exhaling more fully, releasing your forehead, shoulders, back, neck, jaw, and hands. Reach your arms up to the ceiling, or curl forward and reach down to the floor. If this type of movement isn't appropriate for the setting, shift in your seat and lengthen your spine.

Mental Time Away

Converging deadlines can trigger the stress response. Instead of worrying about everything that is on your plate, give yourself a mental break by:

- Prioritizing your task list;
- Hyper-focusing on one task at a time; and
- Following through, getting it done before mentally moving on to the next task.

Like the mechanism that trips a circuit breaker when you use too many appliances, being present interrupts the current of stress by suspending the cascade of conclusions that make challenging circumstances seem threatening, severe, and overwhelming. Being present, which is focusing on the moment as it occurs, allows you to shift from fight-or-flight to problem solving.

Step 2: Shift Your Focus

In times of stress, it is easy to get stuck, leading to thoughts and behaviors that become circular, obsessive, or otherwise out of whack. Once you have become present, consider shifting your focus with one or more of the following strategies:

Shift Your Thinking

Shifting your focus often means looking at a problem differently or reevaluating the strategy. Talk your challenge through with a friend or colleague, or shift to another task on your to-do list such as responding to email or organizing your desk.

Shift Within Your Type

This is where heightening self-awareness comes into play, and particularly your Type. Every person has a pre-wired stress response that is an overdoing of information-gathering or decision-making. Identify your pre-wired stress response, and then do the other.[6]

Shift Your World

This strategy refers to shifting between Extraversion and Introversion.[7] Identify whether you have had too much time "on" with people or too much time alone. Then, make the shift to the other.

---

6. *See* QUENK, *supra* note 4.
7. *Id.*

Step 3: Check Your Gut

If you are still feeling stress after you have implemented the strategies described in Steps 1 and 2, it is time for a gut check. Consider whether you are avoiding an important issue. Do you need to talk with a more senior lawyer and get feedback on a project that didn't go well? Is it time to have a difficult conversation, make a hard decision, or accept a distasteful situation that you worked hard to prevent, but has become a reality? Resisting the inevitable has an exponential effect on stress. Remember, it's not the problem, but how you deal with it that counts. Find those twenty seconds of courage and act.

Finally, remember the importance of self-care routines? Consider whether your life lends itself to short-circuiting stress preemptively. If so, try these three simple steps at the beginning or end of your day so that you gain insight into your own triggers, increase calm and focus, and become more agile in short-circuiting stress.

Conclusion

Your first year of law practice is likely to be both exciting and scary at the same time. To do more than survive—to thrive—you need to keep your wits about you. The strategies in this chapter provide you with the tools for self-care that will ensure that you are able to do your best. Yes, you will be challenged. But that's the fun of practicing law and, yes, you are up to the challenge.

Chapter 16

Getting, Accepting, and Retaining Feedback

Laura S. Norman*

"We all need people who will give us feedback. That's how we improve."

— **Bill Gates**

Most people would agree that getting feedback is a critical component of learning. Yet many of us approach reviews by others of our work or our behavior with a combination of fear, anxiety, and dread. That fear, anxiety, and dread arise from several causes. Although we will all readily agree "nobody is perfect," we do not really like to admit our own failings, much less be told about them by somebody else. We also do not like being told something about ourselves which we recognize to be true but of which we were not previously

---

*   President of LSN Consulting Ltd.

aware (our so-called "blind spots") or to discover other people see things about us that we think we have kept hidden. In addition, many of the people we receive feedback from have little to no understanding of how to give difficult feedback in a useful way. As a result, they often try to avoid doing so until what may start out as a minor problem has escalated to a major issue from the giver's perspective, which makes any "truths" they are trying to communicate that much harder to hear and receive. This chapter will address the best ways for new attorneys to become more comfortable getting feedback, to really hear and assimilate the quality feedback received, and to learn how to solicit feedback that will enhance professional growth and development.

What Is Feedback?

The *Oxford English Dictionary* defines feedback as "[i]nformation about reactions to a product, a person's performance of a task, etc. which is used as a basis for improvement." It is the communication by one or more persons to another person of information about the effect of that person's words, behavior, or performance on those around him or her. Feedback can consist of information that: (a) is known to the person receiving it; (b) is not known to the person receiving it but known to others; or (c) causes the person receiving it to see or understand something about him or herself that was not consciously known previously.

Feedback is one of the most important tools we use to teach, to learn, to grow, and to encourage others to learn, grow, and improve. Feedback generally falls into three basic categories:

- **Positive feedback:** Feedback that affirms someone's words, work, or behavior. Its purpose is to show someone appreciation, affirm someone's value to the group, and reinforce wanted behaviors. Almost everyone enjoys getting positive feedback. When getting it, make sure to take it in and appreciate its value in confirming you are on the right path.

- **Corrective feedback**: Feedback that points out errors or problems with someone's words, work, or behavior. Its purpose is to eliminate unwanted behavior, improve performance, and make the receiver more productive and effective. Corrective feedback is the feedback we often think of as "negative" because it is critical of our work or behavior, but it is most important to new attorneys to help you shed bad habits and learn best practices.

- **Clarifying feedback**: Feedback in which the listener tells or "feeds back" to the speaker the listener's understanding of what the speaker has said. Its purpose is to make sure the speaker and the listener are on the same page, that the listener understands what the speaker is saying and what the speaker wants, and to resolve any possible misunderstandings or confusion. Clarifying feedback is the feedback all attorneys who want to do well employ frequently to make sure they understand the expectations of their supervisors, colleagues, clients, opposing counsel and his/her clients, and judges.

Why Receiving Feedback Is Often Hard

Even quality corrective feedback, feedback given with the best of intentions, in the safest psychological environment from a person who truly has your best interests at heart, can be painful to hear. It can be unsettling and distressing to discover things about ourselves that we did not know, or did not know others knew about us, or to have to confront our shortcomings. Yet most people will admit the most important lessons they have learned in life were painful in some way. In her book, *In the Freud Archives*,[1] Janet Malcolm writes, "The unexamined life may not be worth living, but the examined life is impossible to live for more than a few moments at a time." While that may be true, it is also true that the more we know about ourselves and the more we allow other people to know about us, the more likely it will be that at the end of any communication, we will have an accurate sense of what the other person is trying to communicate to us, and they will understand what we are trying to communicate to them, even if we do not agree.

Feedback meant to be corrective and constructive is often perceived by the receiver negatively. We naturally want to reject it because it undermines our sense of self. We may think the advice is bad or wrong. We don't like the person giving it to us or mistrust their motives for doing so. It's confusing or makes us uncomfortable. The person giving the "feedback" is not doing it to help us improve but to judge us or assert his or her power in the relationship. The feedback is about something we don't think we can change. All of those things may be true and are good reasons to disregard the feedback, but there also may be a grain or more than a grain of truth in what we are being told, and that truth may be something that we need to pay attention to, something that can truly improve our performance and productivity and even change our lives.

Sheila Heen, the co-author of *Difficult Conversations: How to Discuss What Matters Most*[2] and a lecturer in law at Harvard Law School associated with the Harvard Negotiating

---

1. JANET MALCOLM, IN THE FREUD ARCHIVES (1997), at 29.
2. DOUGLAS STONE, BRUCE PATTON & SHEILA HEEN, DIFFICULT CONVERSATIONS: HOW TO DISCUSS WHAT MATTERS MOST (2010).

Project, identifies three "trigger reactions" to feedback in her TED Talk "How to Use Others' Feedback to Learn and Grow." These trigger reactions can prevent us from learning from the feedback we receive.

The first trigger reaction Heen calls the "Truth Trigger"—is the feedback true? Is it accurate? Do we think the advice is good advice? We want to reject hearing "bad" things about ourselves so we look for ways to discount or disregard feedback we perceive as negative. However, even if we don't think the feedback is true or accurate or good advice, we need to look for something we can learn from it, even if it is only information about the giver and how best to interact with that person going forward to avoid similar problems. In addition, the attorneys giving you feedback on your legal work or professional conduct have both more knowledge and experience than you on the subject at hand and a much better understanding of the expectations of their clients. For these reasons alone, you should assume their feedback is valid and worth paying attention to, absent specific evidence to the contrary.

The second trigger reaction Heen refers to as the "Relationship Trigger." Our reaction to feedback varies significantly based upon our relationship with the person giving it to us. We may pay more or less attention to what is being said based on who the feedback giver is. It is therefore important to try to separate the substance of the feedback from the person giving it. Look for what is important about what is being said separately from who is saying it.

The third trigger reaction is the "Identity Trigger." It is our emotional reaction to the feedback we are given. It is how the feedback affects the story we tell ourselves about who we are. The more the feedback conflicts or impacts the story we tell about ourselves, the more intense our reaction will be. Nonetheless, people differ enormously in how they respond to the feedback they are given. Some people are more or less impervious to negative feedback. Others perceive the most minor criticism as a death blow. Where you fall on the emotional scale has positive and negative effects on your ability to benefit from the feedback. Therefore, try to determine the actual significance of the feedback you are given. Is your complained of behavior equivalent to felony murder or is it really just a traffic violation or something in between? The giver may perceive the issue as much more significant than you do, or much less. That doesn't make either of you right or wrong, but understanding what is important to your supervising attorneys or to the client, whether or not it seems all that important to you, is necessary for you to develop a successful working relationship with them. Conversely, you don't want to be seen as overreacting to something a supervising attorney sees as a minor issue as that will deter him or her from giving you feedback in the future.

How to Receive Feedback to Make It Hurt Less and Be More Useful

When receiving feedback, try to keep the following things in mind:

- **Look for any truths or useful information.** Almost all feedback contains something that can be of value to you.

- **Be aware in evaluating the feedback you receive that all feedback consists of some of the giver's projections, implicit biases, and worldview.**

  - Listen to the words more than the person speaking those words;

  - Listen to the content of what is being said more than the words spoken; and

- Try to understand the speaker's real underlying concerns.

- **Understand your own emotional reactions to criticism.** Are you extremely sensitive or do things just roll off your back? Does your reaction align with the giver's view of the significance of the problem? Be aware of differences.

- **Be an active listener.**

  - Listen without planning your response. Focus on understanding what is being said, not what you are going to say. Think about it as trying to write the answer to a complaint when you haven't read the entire document. You need the whole picture before you can formulate an effective response, so do not interrupt.

  - Be aware of your responses. Show in your body language and attitude that what the other person has to say matters to you.

  - Be open to new ideas, to different ways of thinking about how you do things.

- **Provide clarifying feedback.** Once you have allowed the giver to provide you feedback, repeat your understanding of what he or she has said to make sure you got the message, and clarify any points that you found confusing or unclear.

- **Be willing to own your mistakes.**

  - Take responsibility for those aspects of the feedback you know to be true before you defend those aspects with which you may disagree or feel the need to explain or to offer facts or circumstances that may put the complained of behavior in a different light.

- Try not to be defensive or throw someone else (a paralegal, another associate, or a legal secretary) under the bus. You alone are responsible for your work product and will earn respect by displaying that attitude.

- **Takeaways.** Make sure, before the discussion is over, to confirm your takeaways from the discussion; specific things you need to do, changes you need to make, and check if the supervising attorney has any additional suggestions. If you feel like you do not have the specific skills necessary to implement the changes suggested, then find out how you can acquire those skills.

- **Give yourself time and space to reflect.** After receiving difficult feedback, take time and space to reflect on what has been said, the value it has for you, and the consequences of following or ignoring the advice. Then you will be in a position to decide what you are going to do because of it.

- **Get another opinion.** Before you reject feedback, consider talking to your mentor, another colleague, or a trusted friend to get another opinion.

- **Remember to follow up.** After implementing the changes suggested to you by a supervising attorney, check in to make sure he or she is satisfied with the changes you have made.

How to Solicit Feedback

Senior attorneys are often under stress to meet deadlines, close deals, or please difficult clients, so they often do not have the time or the energy to give junior attorneys the meaningful feedback that they need or desire. That does not mean, however, that you cannot find ways to get feedback on your performance. It means you need to take a proactive approach to getting it.

While the best feedback is that given as close in time as possible to the performance or completion of the task, you are not likely to get useful feedback or have a constructive discussion when your supervising attorney is angry, tired, or overwhelmed with work. Therefore, when seeking feedback, try to find the times during the day or the week when your supervising attorney is able to talk to you without interruption and in a calm environment. If you plan ahead by setting up a brief check-in meeting, you are more likely to get the focused attention of your supervising attorney.

The most valuable feedback is specific. If your supervising attorney's feedback is vague or unclear, ask for specific examples and suggestions for ways to correct the problem or get additional help. If a supervising attorney revises a document you produced and does not have time to discuss the changes with you, run a black-line and review the changes yourself. Make sure you understand why the changes were made. Try to find a time after the deal is closed or the deadline has passed to discuss the changes that you do not understand or have questions about with your supervising attorney. If your supervising attorney is unavailable, try reviewing the changes with your mentor or another, more senior associate.

Make sure you understand the difference between the supervising attorney's expectations and what you produced or how you performed. If it turns out that you did not understand the supervising attorney's expectations, try to figure out why that happened. Where did the failure in communication occur? What could you have done so that failure in communication did not happen? Are there things you could ask your supervising attorney to do going forward that would help you prevent the problem from reoccurring? As a junior associate, you will be dealing with multiple attorneys with different styles and manner of doing things. You will need to learn to adapt to those varying demands. You need to find out when you are given an assignment exactly what that particular assigning attorney expects to receive back.

Unfortunately, you are likely to run across one or two senior attorneys in your career who will decide it is easier not to work with you again rather than to spend the time to give you feedback on an assignment that did not meet their expectations. If that happens, you are getting feedback, but it is neither clear nor useful. Consider trying to have a conversation with that attorney, indicating that you would like to do more work with them, but you have not received any assignments from them lately. If the reason is that there were problems with your previous work, you'd like to discuss what those problems were and be given an opportunity to fix them. You may or may not find out what the problem is, but if you don't ask, you will definitely not find out or find out when it is too late to fix.

Finally, pay attention. While not technically feedback, all your interactions with other attorneys and clients are potential learning opportunities. When you are invited to sit in on a call or go to a meeting, do not spend your time texting or reading emails just because you do not have an assigned role or do not yet know what role you will be playing. First, it really annoys clients who are paying for your time and your supervising attorney who has asked you to be there for a reason. Watch what is going on and being said. What are the underlying issues and concerns? What don't you understand? Whose negotiating style do you like? Whose arguments were the most persuasive? How are the power dynamics affecting the conversation? Then, after the meeting or call, you can ask questions about the things you did not understand, or find out the reasons why certain issues were resolved in a certain way. When the next assignment on the project comes up, you will have a better understanding of the context and will be more likely to do a better job and get positive feedback on your work.

Takeaways

Although feedback can be painful, it is a vital part of our professional and personal growth. We need to learn to at least tolerate, if not embrace, hearing what the people with whom we work and to whom we report think about our behavior and performance. We need to learn to appreciate when other people provide corrective feedback because it can reduce our blind spots and help us become more effective as professionals and people. We need to develop the habit of giving clarifying feedback to make sure we understand other people's intentions and expectations. Giving and receiving feedback with respect and in good faith increases our ability to hear and be heard by our colleagues and clients and is an essential part of being able to deliver quality legal services.

Chapter 17

Your First Performance Review

Sharon Meit Abrahams, Ed.D.[*]

What Is a Performance Review?

All businesses, and yes, law firms are businesses, need to have a way to measure an employee's success and achievements on the job. This is even more important for law firms because the partners are looking at associates with the thought of making them partners in the future. Through the performance process, firms measure associates against each other to rank them on the track to partnership. This sounds harsh, but it is the reality.

From your point of view, the review process is the time when you learn how you are doing at the firm and if you are, indeed, on track to partnership. The process is also supposed to be a time for you to receive feedback and get constructive advice on how to grow in your role. The review

---

[*]   Director of Professional Development/Diversity & Inclusion, Foley & Lardner LLP.

process is also critical for businesses and law firms to determine compensation and bonuses.

One of the questions that you should always ask during a job interview is "How does this firm measure success?" The review process is the "how" even if the interviewer does not realize it. You should ask about the review process because it gives insight to the firm's culture and how the firm treats its associates, and it outlines your path to success in the firm. Learning who plays what role in the process will allow you to find the right people to help you in your career. Gaining this insight will give you a leg up in preparing for the review as well. This chapter discusses basic, even generic, information about review processes. It is your responsibility to get the specific details from your firm.

Whether your firm does reviews once or twice a year, you should embrace the process. A review should give you feedback on how you are doing with developing your substantive knowledge as well as your "lawyering" skills. Unlike businesses, most firms do not provide feedback throughout the year or on a case-by-case basis, so at times you might wonder how you are doing in relation to your peers. In a perfect world, you should be receiving feedback on individual work product or at the end of a matter, but as this is time that cannot typically be billed, partners often skip the opportunity to provide it.

The Review Process: Data Collection

There are two parts to the review process. The first is to collect data about the person being reviewed and the second is to deliver that feedback to the individual. Each work environment is unique, so what is explained here is a common structure; your firm may augment its process.

Step one is gathering information about your performance. This can be objective information such as hours, which can include billable work, pro bono activities, and non-billable hours. Your firm will give you the parameters of what is being calculated. Employers also collect more subjective information about your skills, abilities, knowledge, and attitude. The skills, abilities, and knowledge may also be called competencies, which will be addressed later.

Each person you do work for will be given an opportunity to share their experience working with you. Your firm will give the attorney a document to complete that is either online through an evaluation system or as a paper form to complete. Note, if your employer is still using paper forms, this might give insight into other critical processes that have not been updated. The questions they answer vary from employer to employer so ask for a copy of the form or look for it on your firm's intranet if they have a professional development page or section. A sample of common questions follow:

1. How much work has this associate done for you? Extensive, moderate, or occasional.

2. What was the complexity of the work? Describe the nature of the work performed.

3. Did the associate produce work timely?

4. Would you choose to work with this associate again?

5. Does this associate show aptitude in:

    a. Analysis

    b. Judgment

    c. Written communication

    d. Oral communication

    e. Task and/or project management

Some forms will have spaces for narrative responses to questions or statements like: Describe areas in which the associate excels or needs improvement. They might also be asked their opinion of an associate's ability to maintain enough work to be a partner. No matter the form, the key is that each person you have worked with in the past six to twelve months gets a chance to comment on your performance whether it is positive feedback or not.

For your benefit, it is a good habit to remind the people you have worked for about the work you did for them, especially if it has been longer than six months. Just before or when the review process begins, send key attorneys a summary of the work you did for them and include the quantitative value as well as anything that stands out about the experience. Send them any client emails you have received that demonstrate the quality of the work you did or the relationships you have built. You should not be surprised if you see your exact words cut and pasted into the evaluation form so make sure it is well written and gives good detail.

Depending on the firm, your department or practice group might also gather data via team meetings in which partners and other supervising attorneys talk about the people being evaluated. These meetings allow partners and supervising attorneys to provide information that they are reluctant to write on the evaluation form. In some firms, partners worry that their honesty on an evaluation form will lead to the associate no longer being willing to work with them. Of course this is not usually the case, but it still happens. Ask if your firm has these types of meetings so you know whom to follow up with preemptively if you think they might make negative comments about you. Try to respectfully remind them of the positive work you have done so they do not focus solely on the one screw-up. (And yes, you will have some screw-ups your first year.)

Self-Evaluation

You might be asked to complete a self-evaluation as part of the review process. This is a wonderful opportunity and should not be passed up. If your firm does not give you structure, such as a form to complete or questions to answer, then consider the following. Busy attorneys are not interested in reading your life story and they have limited time, so be concise and as brief as possible. This being said, what you write can affect your compensation and bonus as well as how the partners view you going forward so invest time in writing this document. You should cover the following:

1. List billable activities and highlight assignments that are exceptional or significant in some way.

2. Address if your billable time was considerably high or low and why.

3. Describe pro bono work and what you learned.

4. Discuss non-billable work that helped raise the firm's or your profile (i.e., community activities).

5. Outline business development initiatives that you worked on and the outcome.

6. Include firm citizenship activities like recruiting or mentoring.

As mentioned before, this is a generic list of topics you could address. Your firm should give you a list of what they want to learn from you. If the firm does not have a list of topics, ask associates what they have included in the past and ask partners what they would like to know about your practice.

Do not be redundant in your self-evaluation, meaning there is no need to repeat what the reviewer already has, such as your billable hours and pro bono work. Focus on important factors such as the quantitative or qualitative value of the work or how a client interaction led to more work. To help you determine what to write about, start keeping a log or diary of unique, highly stressful, overly complex, or otherwise uncommon occurrences throughout the year (or review period if less than a year). Jot down the attorneys and clients involved. Describe how the experience was distinctive or unusual and how your knowledge grew or skills developed because of it. Include client emails if they support the statements you are making. If you had an unfortunate personal or family situation that impacted your workload, this is also the place to explain, without too much detail (HIPAA rules apply). On a positive note, also mention if you got married, had a child, or other happy events that may have affected your availability for work.

Once you have submitted your self-evaluation and all the people participating in your evaluation have submitted their reviews, the person assigned to be your reviewer will compile a final evaluation form including the objective data. Depending on your firm's culture, you may or may not see the original individual feedback, only a summary. This final review will likely be studied by multiple people in your firm, such as your practice group leader, department head, or mentor. If your firm has a review committee, then this would be read by individuals on the committee as well. And finally, if your firm has a partner promotion committee, then your review will be viewed by them as well. This is why what you write for your self-evaluation and how you write it is so important.

The Review Process: The Meeting

Ideally, the reviewer will set an appointment for the review and provide you the written review document at least twenty-four hours in advance of the meeting so you have time to digest it and formulate appropriate questions. If this is not standard where you work, ask for a copy of your review anyway as it will help you prepare for the meeting. If this is not an option, still write down your questions and concerns.

If you receive the written review prior to the meeting, read it and immediately note your thoughts and emotions. Walk away. Come back a little later and read it again. If your review is filled with glowing comments, then you are a superstar and probably have little to worry about. Do not be led astray and think there is nothing you should ask about. Use your meeting time to ask questions about what the practice group, department, or firm's expectations are related to making partner. Talk about areas of law you would like to expand into or specific partners you would like to work with. Ask to work with certain clients and on special projects. If you are on the "A-list," take advantage of your good fortune and ask for what you want and need to continue on this trajectory.

If your review catches you off guard and you read about areas that need improvement, make notes to discuss those during the meeting. Questions to ask during the meeting should focus on areas for more training and mentoring. You can inquire about resources that are available to you. Ask if they will send you outside the firm to receive training or will assign someone to work with you internally. Query those in attendance how they recommend you could make adjustments. Be sure to ask them for guidance on what they think is most important to work on and how long you will have to demonstrate improvement. In some cases, your review will double as a performance improvement plan and what your supervising attorney(s) want to see accomplished will be included.

Some firms require more than two people to be present in a review, even if the review is all positive. This means that in addition to the reviewer and you, others attending might include your mentor, practice leader, office head, or someone from the professional development or human resources department. The person giving you the review should be prepared and well trained on how to deliver reviews; unfortunately, many partners are not, so your experience may not match exactly what is described here.

The scheduled meeting is often in a partner's office, but a better location is a conference room; if you feel comfortable, ask for it to be moved to a conference room. At the meeting, the reviewer would deliver the summary of all the reviews, letting you know how people view your work. This includes the overall quality, writing style, and substance of your actual work product. You will also receive feedback on how you are viewed by others on issues such as whether you are sufficiently responsive, a team player, or have a "go-to" attitude. You should be told if you are meeting expectations or if there are changes you need to implement.

If you receive constructive criticism during your review, you should not consider it a "poor review," but rather an opportunity to embrace the feedback and make adjustments. If the reviewer comments on behaviors or work products that need improvement, ask for specific examples. It is hard to bake a better cake if you do not know what is wrong with the cake. Is it too dry or is it tasteless? Through examples you will learn if you are lacking knowledge or a skill. Since some partners are reluctant to give negative feedback, press the reviewer to tell you who has the stated issue so you can work with that person to make the necessary changes. Though the partner might be put off when you initially approach him or her, he or she will soon learn that you are trying to be a better attorney and you need their direct input.

You may work for a firm that does not have a formal review process, or that somehow you fell through the cracks and never received a review meeting. This can happen so be brave and speak up. If you fell through the cracks, do not wait too long before inquiring about your meeting. It is possible a partner was out of town or in trial and the lack of a review meeting was simply an oversight. Raise it with your mentor or practice lead, and they will make sure the session gets scheduled and conducted.

Some firms are moving away from yearly reviews to more frequent "just in time" feedback throughout the year. However, even if your firm does not have a formal review process, do not settle for not getting a review. Ask the attorneys you work for to give you feedback either in a group setting (take them to lunch!) or individually. The information you receive will help you plan your career goals and decide what skills you need to work on as well as give you, hopefully, a boost in the right direction.

Competencies

A key aspect of the review process is measuring your performance against your firm's competencies or benchmarks. Competencies are the expected skills, abilities, or knowledge you should have at a certain level in your career. Benchmarks are activities or tasks that you have achieved, and demonstrated mastery of, through your work. Typically, competencies and/or benchmarks are published by the firm as an online document or in a professional development manual and shared with new associates and lateral hires. Most mid- to large-size firms have competencies/benchmarks that cover general firm skills with separate ones that cover specific practice area expectations.

Sample general competencies would be your analytical skills, judgment, writing, and communication abilities. Practice area skills would be based on your abilities around being a litigator, transactional attorney, or intellectual property attorney, among others. Sample benchmarks would be taking or defending depositions, as well as handling parts of a matter with little or no supervision. If your firm does not have published competencies or benchmarks, then you need to talk to your mentor, supervising attorney(s), or practice leaders to find out what they will be measuring at your performance review.

Setting Goals for Your Future

Ultimately, you are responsible for your own career. Whether you work for a large or small firm, whether they have a review process or competencies, you need to hold yourself accountable for progressing in your practice. It has been well established that goal-setting helps individuals stay on track to make their professional dreams come true. Goals are simple to create in your mind and tougher to see through in reality. If you follow the SMART model, you will create goals that are Specific, Measurable, Attainable, Results-oriented, and within a Timeframe. Discuss goals with the attorneys involved in your performance review process to demonstrate your dedication to the position, the team, and the firm.

When developing your goals, answer the following three questions:

1. What is your goal? It is important to articulate the goal(s) you have with the people around you. It has been proven that by stating a goal out loud you are making a commitment to yourself and others.

2. Why is this your goal? By answering "why" you will understand your motivation, which effects your commitment to attaining the goal.

3. How will I achieve this goal? This is where the rubber hits the road: if you do not know how to move forward, you will flounder.

All three of these questions can and should be discussed with the attorneys you work for and those whose opinion you respect.

You will be nervous each and every time you receive a performance review. Even partners who have practiced over twenty years feel that pang in their stomach when they meet with firm leaders to discuss how they are doing. Going into the review prepared and understanding the value of the feedback will propel the meeting into a highly productive use of your time. Embrace the experience.

Chapter 18

When Is It Time to Leave Your Firm?

Julie Lehrman[*]

Introduction

Knowing when to leave your firm, or whether to leave the practice of law, involves a lot of soul-searching. Far too many associates bounce from one firm to another without thinking deeply about what they want, or how a new firm might change or improve their situation. This is a mistake.

It is incredibly important to remember that if you are to land somewhere where you will be happy, you must a) identify what is making you unhappy, and b) identify what will make you happy. It is also important to leave open the possibility that you don't enjoy practicing law. When you are trying to figure out your next move, it is imperative that you be painfully honest with yourself.

Within the first few years of practice, solid associates will go through a process of asking themselves some hard ques-

---

[*]   Founding Member of North Star Attorney Search, LLC.

tions about who they are and what they want their practice to look like. Sometimes, you are just in a bad situation. This happens. However, when you find yourself in bad situation after bad situation, you may need to ask yourself whether perhaps you just don't like the practice of law.

When Your Current Firm Is a Bad Fit

There are times when, no matter how much you love your firm, your practice area, and the people you work with, it might be time to move on. Sometimes these things are beyond your control. Sometimes, you are just in the wrong firm or practice area. It is very important to have your antennae up for situations that may mean it is time to start your search.

Poor Reviews/Poor Relationships with Partners

I once had an associate come to see me who just wanted to talk. She loved her firm, loved her colleagues, and loved her work. There was, however, one problem. She kept getting assigned to a partner who didn't seem to like her and gave her mediocre reviews.

This associate didn't have much control over who she was assigned to. It was up to each associate to approach partners for work, and the partners she liked and wanted to work for already had associates they went to regularly. Because the other associates made sure they were busy with partners they liked, she was the one who was usually available when this partner needed something, and was asked to do his work. She kept hoping the other partners would have work for her so that she could stay busy, but it wasn't happening.

Many firms have that one partner no one wants to work for. Some firms handle this situation better than others. If you go to a firm where work is distributed by an assignment partner, you will be rotated through different partners and different assignments. The result is that all the associates share the more enjoyable partners, as well as the difficult ones. However, if you are responsible for creating relationships with partners who will keep you busy, you could find yourself in this situation, and it can be hard to extract yourself. If you don't see a way out, it could be time to start looking for an opportunity where you have more control over the partners you work with. In interviews with other firms, be sure to ask how work will be assigned, and whether the position entails working with a particular partner or partners. If so, make sure to spend as much time as you can with them before accepting an offer to join the firm.

Similarly, some firms handle the giving of bad news better than others. Often, I have seen firms give an associate a gentle nudge toward the door in the hopes that the associate will take the hint and move on. Some firms are subtle to the point that the associate does not realize she is being nudged. If your firm has told you that they don't see you making partner, or they have indicated more than once that you are not progressing as you should, you might be getting a nudge, and you should see what else is out there.

By the same token, some associates do not receive bad news well. If you are being given the same criticisms by multiple partners, it is time to do some soul-searching. You will need to put in some time alleviating their concerns and addressing the issues they are raising with you. If you are truly convinced that their criticisms are unfair or unfounded, you may think about moving to a different type of practice (non–law firm, for example), or leaving the practice of law altogether.

Partners Leaving

Partners come and go all the time, especially in large firms. But when a partner who is significant to your practice leaves, you must ask yourself whether and how it might affect you. The worst situation is when a work provider partner (or partners) leaves, takes a few associates to the new firm, and leaves you behind. Never forget that law firms are businesses, and when a profit-generating partner leaves and takes their clients with them (as they inevitably do), the firm may not be able to keep you on. When a partner who has been providing work to you leaves, you must find out whether there will be work enough to sustain you. You can ask a partner you trust, or your professional development coordinator (if your firm has one). It will be a delicate conversation, but it is in your interest to have it. If the firm indicates (or you sense) that they are not sure about your future now that the work is gone, it is time to start talking to other firms.

Firm Merger/Changes in Management

Similarly, it is important to pay attention to whether partners are leaving after a merger or a change in management. Some attrition is inevitable, so a few partners departing is not necessarily cause for alarm. However, if you notice a trend of many partners from different groups leaving the firm over a short period of time, you will want to start looking for somewhere more stable. It is important to pay attention and watch for signs of whether the changes are being well received. If you are close with a partner in the firm, or with a high-placed administrator who is familiar with the business of the firm, you should pick their brain about what the changes might mean for you. And, as mentioned above, keep an eye out for more than a few partners leaving, even if they are in other groups.

When Your Current Practice Area Is a Bad Fit

There is another possibility—that you are simply in the wrong practice area. Changing practice areas can be tough if the transition doesn't make sense for the firm; however, in some scenarios it is doable (corporate law to bankruptcy law is a common transition, as are tax to employee benefits, and litigation to employment law). Understand that if you try and change practice areas by going to another firm, the firm is essentially taking you on as an entry-level attorney, with all the expense that entails for them. Firms generally dislike hiring an associate with several years experience in one area but no training in the target area. Therefore, the ideal situation is when you can change practice areas within your own firm.

If you can convince your firm to let you transition to another practice area, this is probably the most painless way to transition. However, you need to propose something that makes sense for your firm, and, to do this, you need to pay attention to market trends. What does your firm need? Where are they facing hiring challenges? How does your skill set translate to the firm's needs?

Additionally, transitioning to another practice area can be politically difficult. Talk to the target partners before you discuss your idea with the partners you work for now. If you can, talk to a legal recruiter, and to the professional development professionals at your firm. You don't want to tread on the toes of the lawyers you work for before you have a new position lined up.

When You Don't Become (or Want to Become) a Partner in Your Current Law Firm

As a legal recruiter, I get many questions from junior lawyers, students, and people who are contemplating law school who envision themselves going to a large, prestigious firm and eventually becoming partner. I tell them all the same thing: to truly be successful at a large law firm (or any law firm, really), you have to do more than be good at practicing law. You have to LOVE it. You need to be someone whose mind is always thinking about your clients, their problems, and their solutions. The truly successful partners I know have spent years throwing themselves into what they do. They wake up in the morning thinking about the law. They go on vacation and think about the law (and sneak off to send emails). Someone once said that being a law partner is like a pie-eating contest in which the prize is more pie. If you are someone who likes the law, but isn't prepared to throw your heart and soul into your job for probably twenty years (when you can maybe start to relax), you may want to re-think whether you have the level of commitment required to become a big firm partner. You must also enjoy building a client base—an important component of partnership no matter what size your firm. Many lawyers do not enjoy the process of cultivating clients, which can be seen as essentially a type of sales. This may sound harsh, and I don't mean it to be. It is possible to have a wonderful legal career without living your life in a large law firm. Becoming a law partner is simply not for everyone.

The most obvious option is to become a partner in a smaller law firm. However, it is important to remember that a smaller firm practice isn't necessarily easier than a large one—it's just a different market. You will still need to enjoy cultivating clients (just as important at the smallest firms than at the largest) and maintaining them once you have them. The difference between being a partner in a small firm versus a large firm is that the stakes and pressure are arguably lower, but it is, in most aspects, a very similar job.

Other options are in-house, government, and nonprofit jobs. It is important to understand that once you make either of these career moves, it is very hard to go back to a law firm, so you will want to be very careful before making a jump to any of these. Here's a word about each.

Government jobs can be wonderful, especially if you are in the federal government. They are stable, comfortably paying, and with 9–5 hours. Outside of Washington, D.C., federal jobs are few and far between, and the interview process takes many months, so be prepared for that. If you are looking at state and local positions, just understand that they may be tied to politics (more in some places than others), which means that if the administration changes, or the party in power changes, you may lose your job, or find yourself unhappy and want to leave. And once you're in such a job, it is hard to transition back to the private sector. Networking is just as important when you're working for the government as it is in the private sector.

In-house positions can also be wonderful—just make sure you go to the right one. Not all in-house positions are created equal. Choose a company with a good name and reputation that will allow you to transition to something else if it doesn't work out. Make sure you're getting a variety of skills; there is a stigma against in-house lawyers that they perform only management tasks and farm out all the "real" legal work to outside law firms. It is up to you to ensure that you keep your skills sharp and are performing substantive legal work. Also, do not assume your position will be 9–5. This is a common misconception of in-house positions. If your help is needed on a matter, you will be expected to stay late, perhaps for weeks, just as in a law firm. I can't tell you how many in-house lawyers come to me disappointed because they are making less money but working as hard as they did in a law firm.

Perhaps the most difficult transition to make, and to transition back from, is going to the not-for-profit sector. Generally speaking, transitioning to a not-for-profit position requires experience in that sector. If you manage to get a position in the not-for-profit sector, be aware that the work can be grueling, the resources scant, and the payoffs rare. Like being a law firm partner, you really must love this work, because it is a hard life. If you love it, you won't notice. If you don't, you will burn out quickly. Please be as sure as you can before you make this move.

The common thread with alternate practices of law is that once you make the transition from a law firm to one of these practices, it is very hard to do anything else. Investigate each opportunity and make sure it is the kind of position that will enable you to springboard to another opportunity if it doesn't work out for some reason.

When You Don't Want to Practice Law Anymore

Many, many lawyers practice for a few years and decide to do something else altogether. Lawyering and law school have little in common. Real-world problems experienced by clients are not nearly as exciting as the made-up law school scenarios that were given to us on exams. Corporate culture and the level of commitment required of associates can come as a shock, and the first few years of practicing law can be a period of soul-searching, and also of trying different things. Many lawyers conclude that their heart is truly somewhere else, and that's where they want their energy to be. Once you've changed law firms once or twice and found you're still unhappy, and/or changed practice areas and found you're still unhappy, you may want to ask yourself whether lawyering is for you at all.

Luckily, there are various other careers that make use of a legal skill set without requiring you to practice law in a traditional sense. Many lawyers move to the business side—running businesses or working in corporate compliance. There are careers in legal publishing, law school administration and career services, human resources positions, legal recruiting, and legal administration jobs such as at the ABA and similar organizations. I've seen IP lawyers turn to inventing, corporate lawyers become CEOs, employment lawyers become HR experts, tax lawyers focus on accounting, and all varieties of lawyers turn to politics and lobbying. Having a law degree will only help you in these endeavors.

Starting a Job Search

Don't Wait Until the Last Minute

It is best to get out of a sinking firm before things get really bad. If your firm is about to have a merger that your colleagues seem down about, if your work provider gives you a warning that partners may begin an exodus, if the firm announces that your new practice group manager is someone you don't trust, you need to start looking around. Looking around is just that—you don't commit to anything until you accept an offer. It won't hurt you to see what's out there, and the more time you have, the better. What you don't want is to find yourself in a situation where things have clearly turned for the worse and you need to get out now. Don't wait for that moment. If you do, you will find yourself desperate to find a new situation, and that is not a place you want to be. Start making connections and talking to people as soon as you suspect things may be going awry. Have lunches. Go on interviews. If it turns out that your firm is in better shape than you suspected, you can always back out and decide to stay.

How to Find a Reputable Recruiter

Many lawyers find their next job through a legal recruiter. Probably the best way to find a good one is through a friend's recommendation. Do you have a friend who recently got a great legal job? Ask them if they used a recruiter, and ask for that person's contact information. Sometimes, however, you get a call or an email from a recruiter, and are tempted to respond. Feel free, but make sure to vet that person to make sure they have a good reputation. Go ahead and ask them about their credentials and experience.

- Have they practiced law?
- Where did they practice and for how long?
- How long have they been a legal recruiter?
- What are their relationships like with the law firms in your field?
- Do they work with firms in the city you're targeting?
- Do they understand what you do and have access to firms in your field?
- Have they previously made placements at a firm to which they seek to send you, or had interviews there?
- Do they focus on placing associates and partners in firms, or do they have their finger in many pies, like placing paralegals, assistants, and temps? (A bad sign, generally.)

Have your antennae up, because a really good recruiter can make all the difference, especially when it comes to time to negotiate the terms of your offer. I recommend working with someone with at least five years' experience. If they can't answer basic questions, resent you asking, or ask you for money (reputable recruiters are paid by their law firm clients, not by you), I do not recommend using that recruiter.

Non-Recruiter Resources for Finding a New Position

Working with a recruiter is just one job search tool, and whether you work with a recruiter or not, you should consider several ways of looking for new opportunities when you decide you might want to leave your current firm.

There are, of course, many jobs search websites on which you can find legal jobs, including general sites such as Indeed.com and LinkedIn.com. For federal government jobs, there is www.usajobs.gov, and for in-house legal jobs, you can visit www.acc.com.

For law firms, one of my favorite tools is the website www.martindale.com. You can search law firms by location, size, practice area, and more. Just choose firms that look like they fit your practice, and send them a resume and a cover letter explaining who you are and why you might be a fit for them. They might throw your resume in the trash, but they might not. Not to worry—not all of them need to hire you; one match is all you need.

Don't forget to contact your career services office from law school. Call them up and ask to speak with the counselor who handles alumni. Law schools often have listings that recruiters never see.

Never underestimate the power of networking. Many lawyers get a new job based on the recommendation of a friend. Don't be afraid to ask friends if they can introduce you to someone who handles hiring within their firm.

Conclusion

Deciding what you want your law practice to look like is a soul-searching process to which associates should devote adequate time. As early as after a year or two of practice, sometimes more, you should be asking yourself the hard questions about what you want your life to look like. Too often, associates focus on the work that is in front of them rather than their long-term trajectory. Throughout your first few years as an associate, be asking yourself about what you like, what you don't like, and how you might improve your situation. Doing the hard work up front will lead to a longer, happier, and more successful career.